Dedication

In dedication to all the people in my life and throughout history who strove to live and teach the lessons of love. Your example of what is possible in life has led me in my moments of ignorance and hope.

The Human Experience

VOLUME II
A HEART-CENTRED LIFE

Rae Beecher

Copyright © 2021 Rae Beecher

ISBN #: 978-1-7367228-2-4 (paperback)
ISBN #: 978-1-7367228-3-1 (e-book)

Library of Congress Control Number: 2021905058

All rights reserved. This book or any portion thereof may not be reproduced or used in any manner whatsoever without the express written permission of the publisher except for the use of brief quotations. If utilizing brief quotations reference of the author and work is necessary and cannot be utilized in a manner that indicates or implies Rae Beecher's endorsement or otherwise involvement in the work.

The content of this book is meant to expose and educate the reader. In no way does it replace diagnosis and treatment by a qualified medical practitioner or therapist. Nor does it replace personal judgment and discernment. No expressed or implied guaranteed results or improvement from the use of the recommendations and information can be given or liability taken.

Every known effort has been made to ensure that the websites and links found within the book are accurate as of the time of original publication. However, neither the publisher nor the author can guarantee their continued existence or accuracy.

Editing by Lia Ottaviano.
Cover Art and Interior Formatting by Geoff Borin.
(The sacred geometric symbol found on the cover and within this book is known as Rose of Venus. A representation of the eight-year journey Venus makes with Earth as they travel through the heavens.)

Printed by Lightning Source LLC in the United States of America.

First printing edition 2021.

Publisher: Rae Medicine Woman LLC
PO Box 69
Oroville, WA
98844

www.raemedicinewoman.com

CONTENTS

Prologue
8

Introduction
10

CHAPTER ONE

A Quick Review
14

CHAPTER TWO

Adding a Principle
27

CHAPTER THREE

A Wounded Heart
46

CHAPTER FOUR

Authentic Love
66

CHAPTER FIVE

Understanding Love
77

CHAPTER SIX
Being of Love, The Nature of Love
103

CHAPTER SEVEN
Self-Love
139

CHAPTER EIGHT
Self-Love in Action
161

CHAPTER NINE
Healing and Life's Journey
204

CHAPTER TEN
Manifestation – How it All Works
244

EPILOGUE
Stepping Into a New World
268

Bibliography 270   Acknowledgments 272

About the Author 274

PROLOGUE

Take a journey with me, where we will delve into foreign lands, traveling across unused and forgotten paths. A journey where we will shed light onto another world, another way of life.

This journey is one of healing. It is a path that will lead us to that tender place you might already be able to sense within yourself.

We began this healing journey with Volume One, *What is the Human Experience?*, and the first thing I asked you to do was to sit and breathe. By setting a timer for one minute, I asked you to close your eyes, settle within your seat, and for a single moment, just breathe.

In...

Feeling your lungs expand as air is pulled into your body. The result of this action fills you with the soothing energy of love.

Once your lungs are filled, enjoy the sensation of being connected to the world around you.

PROLOGUE

Out...

With the powerful force of your diaphragm, expel the air that once was in your lungs, and return it to the world around you. With this single act, weave yourself within this world.

As the minute passes just sit with me, feeling your body as it expands and contracts. Know peace within this one minute.

In Volume One, following a single minute of tranquility, I explained what we accomplished. In having you breathe with me, for a single minute, I helped you to uncover a truth: the truth that you are special for no other reason than existing. For being here.

With this simple proof of your worth we started our healing journey. Now it's time to take the next step.

INTRODUCTION

I live in a world, a hidden reality, that has long been sequestered in the shadows. A world where mere moonlight has been our guiding light. While this symbolism may conjure images of ghosts, goblins, and ghouls, I can assure you that while we have remained in the shadows, we do not represent the horrors of the world.

My world is built on love. Now, you may be wondering, if we are beings of love, why we do not reside within the sunlight? The answer is that as beings of love, we embrace ourselves in our entirety—whole-heartedly, as it were. This means embracing our light and our darkness.

In this society, the light of day has become synonymous with all things good, safe, and stable. All that society has rejected has thus been pushed out of sight.

When you live a life as I do, you embrace all of who you are, and all of humanity. As a result, it becomes unsafe to reside in the light and love what others openly hate and reject. We are, however, safe in the darkness, where every facet of life can be found.

This is the world I am about to share with you. As you enter into this new land, I shall pull back the curtain on centuries-old myths and bring the ancient past back to the light. Once you absorb this insight, you can decide for yourself whether or not this way of life is for you.

INTRODUCTION

If you look to history, you will see this sanctuary is not new, but has been a refuge for some time for many faiths and groups of people. People who embrace an element of human life or philosophy, have been historically feared and hated by those living in the sunlight.

The Taoists, who embraced the philosophy of duality, wove their beliefs into Buddhism in order to escape the hatred and systematic eradication led by those of Confucianism. In those days, Taoism was practiced in secret, in the shadows.

Taoism was not the only set of beliefs that was forced into the shadows in order to survive. Those of the Wiccan faith can still recall the history of Salem and the witch trials. Their connection with the Earth, their comfort with their sexuality and feminine power, led them to flee into the night in order to escape the burning pyre.

The same can be said of tribes within the Aztec Empire, tribes like that of my ancestors. Like the Taoists, they hid their beliefs within the faith of the Aztecs, passing down their medicine and healing through their families. This is how I first became a medicine woman—from my father's people.

If we look hundreds of years later, we will see those of the Jewish faith under attack, this time literally concealing themselves in the darkness of attics and basements in order to hide from the Nazi regime and their supporters.

When we look closely at groups of people, we see, again and again, the need for human beings to find solace in the shadows. Whether it was African Americans who traveled by night to get to the free states, or homosexual or otherwise marginalized people, the night has been a place for those who are rejected and persecuted by mainstream culture to find acceptance and prosperity.

Any refugee or persecuted person knows of the safety found within the night. We know that to go without our faith or without our souls would do more harm than the raging armies or hateful clans who hunt us.

They can break bones and bodies, but they can't break our souls, and as time passes their threats weaken and their power shatters. Today, the danger of loving oneself no longer holds the same threats. As you look around today, you'll see that those of us who were once in the shadows have stepped out into the sunlight.

My country offers marriage for all, and equal opportunities for people of any race, creed, color, gender, sexual orientation, and faith. While individuals may scream against these freedoms, those individuals have lost the political power they once had. We do not boast kings or queens, nor do we have inquisitions. While the upholding of our unalienable rights and freedoms may still be a work in process and has yet to reach each individual, these rights are widely acknowledged; more so than in generations past.

What we all have is an unalienable right to whatever life we choose. So, with all that in mind, turn the page as we continue on our healing journey.

CHAPTER 1

A Quick Review

I know more now
than I did before
of space and time
and peace of mind

for in the hour
experienced before
I found the word
I've been searching for

my purpose
my curriculum
I've come to find
lies with the knowledge
that we are human beings

for human means
a combination of all it seems

all I've worked on and
all I've found

Our healing journey began in Volume One of this series by taking a look at our understanding of the human experience. We did this by breaking down the Ten Conclusions that create a human life. These conclusions created a bedrock or framework for your personal philosophy, or your road map to life.

As we learned, our personal philosophy acts as our guide in life. But, if our roadmap is missing key components or has errors, we can end up being led down hazardous paths and on detours that hold us back from our dreams.

Since our personal philosophy addresses our understanding of life, ourselves, and how we weave within this world, it is critical that it is healthy and without false wisdom. So, we have been putting what we know to the test in order to have the best map possible to guide us.

Within this second volume, we will be taking the next step in our reconstruction of our personal philosophy. This healing adventure that you have embarked upon comes with two goals in mind. The first is the act of healing. In this way, you may discover happiness and peace, living life with a calmness within yourself and within the world around you.

The second goal on our healing adventure is to bring us into a new world. This new way of life takes us from a state of survival and elevates us to an existence where we thrive. In order to accomplish these goals, we must not only heal but also uncover the tools necessary to build this world, step into it, and successfully navigate it.

In Volume One, I showed you the world through my eyes. Now I have an even more challenging job: to show you the world through my heart. To help you not only understand but connect on an emotional level with a thriving experience, so that you can have one of your own.

CHAPTER 1: A QUICK REVIEW

The Human Experience

In Volume One we utilized the philosopher Descartes' example of a basket of apples, from *Meditations on First Philosophy*. We learned that hidden gems and rotten truths create our personal philosophy. With this in mind, we took our understanding of life, all the apples that fill our basket, and dumped them out.

Then we started at the very beginning of existence and developed from there, until we had uncovered the world as a whole and reached a greater understanding of how we are here, why we are here, and the intentions behind our existence.

THE HUMAN EXPERIENCE VOL.2

The Ten Conclusions

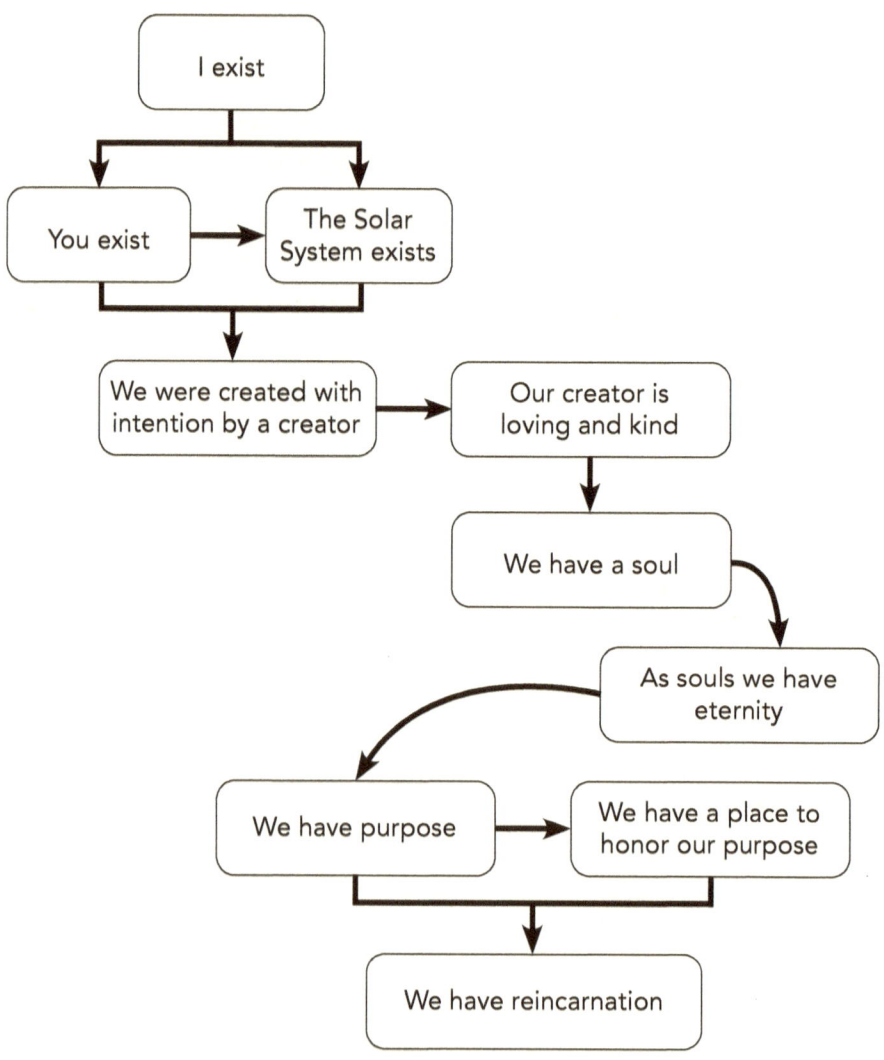

These conclusions created a foundation for each of our personal philosophies. But we didn't stop there. Next, we addressed the Special Truth—the truth that we are each special.

In looking at the impact people have on others and the world at large, from daily conversations, smaller creations (like this book), to major creations (like the wheel), we saw how each of us impact the reality of life. From these observations, we can see just how special each of us are.

We all carry a piece of life's puzzle; we are all critical to the world. Whether our impact is positive or negative depends on how we utilize this Special Truth—if we choose actions and words that come from a place of love and healing, or if we choose actions meant to inflict pain and trauma.

The Victim Mentality

Given all the content that we have explored, and all the new wisdom we will uncover within this volume, it can seem an impossible task to test and re-create our lives. This can be especially difficult if you have been living your life with a victim's mentality.

In life, there is a time and a place for all things. If we carry these things past their moment, we not only place a roadblock in our path, but rather than healing from the pain we encounter in life, we pull unnecessary pain into our lives. The victim's mentality is one of those things that has the potential to be both helpful and harmful.

At the start of your trauma, you are the victim. Someone or something has stepped into your personal world and caused harm. This pain, whether you endured it in childhood or more recently, put you in a place where you were the victim.

There are a number of circumstances that can leave you powerless. Merely being a child can put you in a position where you are unable to escape or avoid pain. The same can be said as an adult when you are outnumbered, facing a weapon, or up against an insurmountable threat.

In these moments, it is important that you see yourself as a victim. You are not responsible for another person's actions or words. You are not responsible for the pain and trauma you've endured—especially when you were a child.

Sometimes, the extremely sad truth is that there was nothing you could have said or done. You were put into a position where you were truly powerless and there was no choice you could have made to solve the situation and spare yourself or those you love from pain.

In viewing yourself from this victim mentality, you can release accountability that isn't yours and acknowledge the wrong done to you. But if you stay too long in this victim mentality, you lose the power to move forward—power that is available to you—and you lose sight of the simple truth that you are responsible for your life.

Once you are free of the perpetrator and in a safe space again, it is time to let go of the victim mentality. That way, you can become responsible and powerful once more. With this power, you have the ability to make changes, heal, and have the last say.

You are now in a position to make decisions about your life. While that person or persons from your past meant to break you and ruin your life, they never actually possessed those abilities. You can push back and reclaim your life. Once you do, you will enjoy the great potential to become any person you desire and to live any life you dream of. You can stop surviving and thrive.

As you read this book, let go of this idea that you are powerless. It is no longer true. Instead, decide what kind of life you want to live, and seek out the knowledge and tools you need to make it so.

With our Ten Conclusions and Special Truth in mind, we kept going and learned more about life. That way you were able to start making changes and utilizing new tools right at the get go.

Energy

An important concept we covered was the impact energy has in our lives. Since we are composed of energy, we are not only influenced by other things made of energy; we can also be the influencer. Due to this fact, we added another layer to our world while also uncovering the basis for a lot of tools we will learn.

Energy is often known in the context of science, but we can take truths uncovered in this field and place them in the context of the metaphysical world. As a result, we can achieve a greater understanding of ancient tools and systems that people have been using for generations.

Einstein's Equation

$E=mc^2$ or   Energy = mass x the speed of light squared
(mass = total amount of matter in an object)

Einstein's equation demonstrates the connection between mass and energy; that energy and mass are effectively the same thing. (mass = very tightly packed energy)

The Law of the Conservation of Energy
Energy cannot be created nor destroyed.

The Law of the Conservation of Mass
Mass is always conserved; no matter what happens to it, the total will be the same amount as when you started.

When paired with Einstein's equation, we discover that what we start with will change but still retain the same amount of energy and mass.

For Example
When we sit around a campfire, we witness a transformation. The logs turn from wood into heat, ash, and steam. What we see, know, and experience changes, but if we were to collect all the ash, heat, and steam at the end of the night, the amount of energy and mass would still be the same as when the evening started.

This transformation of what we know is what we experience each time we use a tool that is built on the premise of energy.

The Metaphysical World + Energy
We often times see ourselves in terms of mass, but as we saw above ($E=mc^2$), mass is made of energy. As beings of energy, we are not only influenced, but can influence other things made of energy. Ergo, tools work even if we are unable to physically see the influence.

For Example

We can pick up, throw, and hear the thud of a stone. The mass of this stone tells us what type of energy we are holding. (Mass = the DNA of energy.)

As beings of energy, we will be influenced by other energetic objects, such as crystals. In this case, the type of crystal determines the manner of influence. As the vibrations (frequency of the stone's energy) from the crystal enters our space, they impact our personal vibrations. These vibrations that we can't see or hear make up the energy that creates our human selves, determining the quality and health of our human bodies. This is why crystal healing is not only real but effective.

Another wonderful example can be found in the foods we eat. We start with a piece of food, raw energy that has taken shape into a specific thing. Once we eat this food, our stomach transforms the energy into fuel for our bodies.

The quality of food will determine what sort of influence the fuel will have on our bodies. Whether we feel sluggish due to sugars and chemicals or re-vitalized due to nutrients and minerals, depends on the quality of the food.

As you can see, energy impacts all elements of human life. Sometimes we see this influence in the context of nutrients, and other times we might not even notice it. Despite the age of many metaphysical tools like crystals, Feng Shui, tarot, and tons more, the connection to energy can be overlooked.

By utilizing the connection between energy and mass, we can not only better understand it, but create wonderful tools to provide healing, guidance, and prosperity. The first set of tools we learned were my Six Safety Tools. Using Shielding, Grounding, Cutting Cords, "Bless me, bless you," Incense and Smudging, and the Elements will help keep us safe, secure, and healthy.

(If you need a recap, check out the last section within Volume One, or head over to my website and check out the articles on each of these tools. www.raemedicinewoman.com/six-safety-tools)

With this multilayered approach to our healing journey, we will build upon the basic bedrock of life and personalize your philosophy in order to support and facilitate your dreams and desires. You will not only learn to thrive but thrive in a way that is of interest to you.

Put it to the Test

As is the case for every book in this series, challenge what you read. If you recall back in Volume One, I introduced the philosophical manner of testing an apple (piece of wisdom) to determine whether you wish to add it to your basket or not.

Step One: Understand
Do you understand what you're reading here, or even what you read elsewhere? Do you understand what you believe, and what others believe?

Step Two: Challenge It
Does what you've read make sense? Do you agree completely or are there some tweaks you need to make?

Step Three: Decide
What will you do with this apple? Does it work with your personal philosophy, or will you leave it on the ground?

I have striven to only include wisdom within these volumes, but I also acknowledge the fact that I am human with a finite understanding. Whether it's a difference in opinion or how to understand and address a situation, put it to the test.

Test what you believe. Test what you hear, see, and are taught by others. Test what you read. Test it because you are worth the time it will take.

When we choose to test the information out there in the world or even the information we've made up in our heads, we remove potential pain from our lives. We also maintain the healthy and helpful nature of our new and improved personal philosophy.

CHAPTER 2

Adding A Principle

as the dark of the world
fell over me
I found a peace within me

for when the darkness
twined with the present light

I felt drawn to the heart
to the love within me
and in that moment

I found a home
I learned a truth
I had forgotten
long ago

that no matter the place
no matter the people
there will always
be a home

for those who are willing
to return to the heart
of all things

With Ten Conclusions, we developed an understanding of human life, and from these conclusions a bedrock for our personal philosophy. While these conclusions are essential for a strong foundation, they lack the glitter, sparkle, and color that represents your personal philosophy. The next step in our healing journey is to choose a principle.

> A PRINCIPLE:
> Defines the manner in which we approach our lives, becoming our chosen lifestyle.

As the title of this book suggests, I have chosen to live my life based on a Heart-Centered Principle. Your principle will not only provide you with more wisdom and tools to navigate your life, but it will also create a world that will support your beliefs.

Many of us know pain through various life experiences and toxic moments. We then carry this pain with us, and it can become chronic, continuing to afflict us until all we see in our future is that pain. That perceived reality about life can threaten our very existence.

Many of us try and do something about our pain. We try to stop it, we try to suppress it, we try to discover a different world, one that is pain free. We address these toxic situations and habits but fail to understand that they are merely symptoms. The root cause of our pain still lives inside of us, and managing our pain can feel like we're fighting a battle that we'll never win.

It is then that life becomes a war, a fight for survival—and there it is, that word "survival." It is our understanding of our lives, the world as a whole, and how and what part we play in the grand scheme of things that dictates what kind of world we enter—it dictates whether we simply survive or live a life in which we thrive.

For many people, dealing with their pain while they are lost can lead to unhealthy techniques. The only thing that seems possible to stop it is to suppress it or fight the trauma of life. But there is another path we can take, one that not only offers a different approach, but requires us to enter into a new understanding. To enter into a new world, where life is not a trauma but a dream, a world where we can eradicate the root cause of our pain.

A Principle

A principle acts like a seed in our lives. The quality and personality of that seed will determine what we cultivate and manifest. When planted into the soil of our bedrock (Ten Conclusions), this seed will flourish. Not only will it develop a specific lifestyle, but it will also stretch into every corner and facet of our lives.

The roots and stems will influence each area of our lives, from home life to work, relationships, and our very understanding of the human experience and the world. Our feelings will begin to change and we will transform and the world we live in will not only change in our eyes but in our hearts, too.

As things currently stand, most people have a fear seed or a Principle of Fear growing from their bedrock. Here, we see not only the rotten apples that we've added to our basket but how we've created these apples. From what we were taught and how we understand the world, this fear seed spreads and influences each moment of our lives.

Thus, cultivating a basket filled with rotten apples and a life that's all about survival. By dumping out our basket of apples and reconstructing our understanding of the human experience, we created a healthy foundation for prosperity. Our next step is to select how we will live our lives.

By choosing this new Heart-Centered Principle, we replace our seed. So, we not only accomplish a healing of our rotten apples (bad habits, false wisdom; the symptoms) but we also accomplish a lasting change. Replacing our seed leaves us with a vibrant rose with kick-ass thorns rather than a weed that strangles everything around it and eventually deprives itself of life.

Love vs Fear

These two different approaches to life will naturally manifest and cultivate certain qualities in our lives. From fear, we discover a natural manifestation of self-judgment, hate, guilt, shame, a victim mentality, and an overall sense of powerlessness. Unfortunately, various societies and rulers over the course of history have utilized this fear seed in order to get what they want, how they want it, when they want it.

Through pictures in the media to propaganda to the very nature of the information they share, these rulers cultivate a powerless society. Because groups of people outnumber a single ruler, and as we've seen in America's history, the power that can be found within a community has the ability to shape a nation. It has the ability to empower the people so they can declare independence and make known the freedoms each human being has and the unalienable right of happiness.

The power of the people, the power of community, only works when a community is bonded. When a ruler sows seeds of fear, shame, and guilt, they create an overall feeling of unworthiness, scarcity, and need for personal safety. Those who live a life of fear can rest easier knowing that the very people they are meant to lead won't be in a position to rise up against them.

Love, on the other hand, is naturally capable of cultivating a very different reality. From love we can find empowerment, a gentleness in spirit towards ourselves, towards others, and towards the world as a whole. We are also able to step back in difficult situations and choose a gentler approach.

The ability to slow down, step back, and observe has led to reconciliations (the reunifying of East and West Berlin), treaties, freedom (India's independence), and even just basic communication. While basic, this communication has played a significant role in the course of historical and personal events.

Choosing a Seed

We see here two principles and the type of flowers that blossom from their seeds. Right now, you have a principle(s) shaping your way of life.

What kind of life are you living? What kind of life would you like to be living?

When I was rebuilding my life, taking what I knew and expanding upon it, I made the decision to approach life from a place of love. It was a challenging decision, because love is something that we know, something that we feel and experience, but not always something we immerse ourselves in.

A life of love—what is that? What does it look like? How do you live it?

The idea of love was beyond my mind's comprehension. As a result, I hesitated, not because I doubted my choice in love, but because love was such a vast and unknown emotion. While I have decided to build my new personal philosophy with a seed of authentic love, I also understand how doing so might be strange for some.

So, on that note, I have provided two scenarios, seen first from the eyes of fear and then from a heart of love. In reading them, you will witness how radically different the nature of life becomes and why we are entering into a new world.

While this world might seem strange and foreign to you, you will also get to see how dreams and hopes are able to flourish when supported by a seed of love.

Example One: A Wounded Human Being

Let us start with an emotionally wounded human being. A human being who has spent their life bringing pain into this world. Maybe this person was your bully in school, your abuser as an adult, or a name or face you saw in the paper. This person has embraced a life that creates problems and challenges for the unity, healing, and potential this world possesses.

This person has also reached a point in their life where there are three distinct paths before them. We all encounter crossroads, and the path we choose leads our life on various types of adventures. Sometimes we see these crossroads and sometimes we can be blind to them. But whether we see them or not, we make a choice that shapes not only our lives but the lives of others.

Path One: Continuation

When this wounded person encounters a crossroads, they have the option to carry on as they have been. This path has them continue to create disharmony in their lives and the lives of those around them, rather than becoming a part of the solution.

Fear

When we look through the eyes of fear, it is easy to see this person as evidence for needing to release control to a domineering society, or to justify the choices of living a sheltered or limiting life. Here, we see how fear can turn a reasonable and practical response—being safe—into an unhealthy and debilitating one.

Love

However, when seen through the eyes and heart of love, we are able to achieve a balance between the practical (locking doors, calling for assistance when needed) and continuing to live our lives. When we see with love we can view this wounded person not only as part of the problem, but also as the product of a wounding life experience and perspective.

This person did not get here all by themselves. Somewhere along the way, an adult or even a child harmed them or taught them an unhealthy idea (rotten apple). In doing so, this person has crafted a personal philosophy that not only harms the world, but also continues to harm their own wounded heart.

Path Two: An End

Another option for our wounded human being is for them to separate themselves from the world. This can happen in a number of ways. They might sequester themselves from others or choose to leave this world permanently. Any number of reasons can cause our wounded person to no longer cause harm.

Fear

When we look through the eyes of fear, we will see the loss of this wounded human being as good. Fear is tenuous because it can disguise itself as a less powerless emotion. So, fear might become an idea of safety and justice, leaving people blind to all of the many facets that exist in this one human being. Just as we each have many facets to who we are, so do they.

But in a moment of fear, it is easier and simpler to only see the problem and be happy that the problem is gone. Or, fear might hide as an emotion, like anger. Anger is a very common outlet for fear. Through anger, this idea of justice or even revenge (you have hurt me, now I will hurt you) can take place.

Love

But when we look through the eyes of love, we see only loss. When we acknowledge the Special Truth, we discover that we are all important to the reality of the world we share. Without this person here, we are going without an essential component in the world.

We also discover within the context of this Special Truth, that sometimes a person's impact is negative rather than positive, and so when we witness the removal of this human being, we see a loss that can trigger a sadness in us. Not only was this person lost to us when they were inflicting pain, but they are still lost to us, and that is a sad truth.

On the practical side of love, we understand that this person could not self-regulate, or they did not know they needed to, and so they were a danger to themselves and others. They were unable to learn the self-control they needed and for the sake of humanity, people needed to step in and take action. So, there is an acknowledgement of a need for change, to not allow the problem to continue, but also an acknowledgment that this is a human being and as such holds something wonderful inside of them that is trapped and blocked from this world.

Path Three: Becoming Part of The Solution

So many things can bring a person down an unhealthy path filled with pain. Ignorance, misinformation, and sustained trauma can wound a person as a child, teenager, or even as an adult.

Fear

When seen through the eyes of fear, a person who has inflicted and brought pain into the world can become less than human. Rather than seeing the path that led this person to this place, we are taught to see only pain and the perpetrator of that pain.

From this perspective, it becomes considerably more challenging for this person to ever change paths and become part of the solution. The reason being, that this perspective requires nothing of people who have been wounded and are living a life based upon fear.

We are taught from a fear-based perspective to hold grudges and condemn another human being when they inflict pain. In our eyes we are taught to forever see them differently. They are now mean or bad people. So, they are never given the opportunity, ability, or permission to heal and, change. To re-align themselves with their true and best selves and reconnect with the world.

Love

Yet when we look through the eyes of love, the potential for healing, growth, and transformation can occur. As things stand, a person who has done wrong and inflicted pain is treated with fear. Sometimes they are even treated with prejudice and ostracism.

Society attempts to dissuade further trauma by telling a person not to hurt people while at the same time inflicting pain. Whether it's jail or social rejection, society is essentially saying, "Do as I say and not as I do." Rather than teaching an alternative path, we beat the "animal," and then are surprised when we get bitten.

But if we can find it in our hearts to accept the possibility of change, we no longer have a person inflicting pain (creating a problem), nor is this person merely gone. Instead, we have another person helping, becoming a voice, an example, and a teacher.

If our newly healed human being can then influence two people who go out into the world and influence two more people, and so on and so forth, the number of supporters grows exponentially. This creates an effective recipe for local and global transformation.

The Impact of Community

All of that said, this potential for change in our "bad" person and within our community hinges on the wounded people, the victims, and on society itself. While it is easy to point the finger at those who break the rules and inflict pain, the situation isn't that simple. We are a community interwoven, creating an ecosystem.

Global change requires participation on all sides—to not only make a change, but to make a lasting change. In order for those lost and wounded souls to become part of the solution, not only must they choose a new path, but so must we.

Rather than inflicting punishment (fear) meant to break or control, we must teach and educate. Since we are interwoven, we all teach and learn from one another. In doing so, we support each other. We not only honor but utilize the community that we share.

To accomplish this truth, we need to be open to the change and growth in those who we have seen cause harm. Thus, we reach a place where we can think and find a charity of heart and spirit within us.

Those whose focus is on feeding their families and keeping them safe have no charity to spare on transformation. So, it's not until we support each other as a community, each of us making strides to change and to grow, that we will be able to grow and transform and truly thrive on a global level.

Example Two: Fault vs. Cause and Effect

Another wonderful example to showcase a lifestyle of love versus fear can be found in the manner in which we approach human error. Currently, we have forgotten the human aspect of our own lives—which is troubling, because the truth that we all share is that we are all human beings.

When I consider what it means to be a human being, I see the potential for growth and prosperity, the potential to show compassion, to know love, to be a community and support system for one another. But I also remember one of our foundational beliefs that creates the bedrock for our personal philosophy.

Conclusion Eight is that we have a purpose. When we take a moment to consider this foundational belief, we can learn more about our lives and grow more than we thought possible.

We discover that on Earth, we are here to learn and to teach. Thus, honoring Conclusion Eight, and also honoring the truth that we are a community. As teachers and students, we can see that in different scenarios, we will play different roles in our lives, and we can also see that when we engage in the role of student or teacher, we can make mistakes.

If we are to deny ourselves the chance to make mistakes, we deny ourselves the chance to be human. If we want to maintain a healthy life we must be conscious of how we address this human aspect in ourselves and others, and if we will address it from a place of fear or from a place of love. So, let's take a look at what these two principles would have us do.

By looking at a playground scuffle we can see the impact that the fear and love seed has had on our lives since childhood. Think back to the days when you were in elementary school and you made a mistake on the playground.

For example, one day you chose to swing on the monkey bars. You started simply, just to warm up those muscles, and then you chose to challenge yourself. To swing, skipping every other bar, then maybe to swing backwards.

Then things got boring. To try something new you chose to climb on top of the monkey bars rather than swinging from bar to bar. (I'm speaking from personal experience here.)

Now, when a recess supervisor sees you sitting on top of the monkey bars, this teacher instructs you to come down. But what follows will determine whether we're dealing with a teacher who lives by and thus sows a seed of fear or a seed of love.

Teacher One

Our first teacher has a personal philosophy built around a seed of fear. From her perspective, she is going to follow the same routine as others do, based on what she's observed and been taught by her family and by society. She is going to march up to you and find you at fault.

You are to blame, you've broken the rules, and now you must pay. There's that idea of punishment for retribution and revenge. Now, you might be sent to sit alone as a "time out," or you might be sent to the principal's office.

All of these things are meant to be unpleasant in order to dissuade you from ever climbing on top of the monkey bars again. What's especially important about this example are the words and the actions that this teacher is going to use to communicate to you that what you did was not ok.

She might use words like, "Listen here young man/lady," or, "You're in big trouble."

But what if there was another scenario that could have played out? What if a different teacher had come and talked to you?

Teacher Two

This second teacher has a personal philosophy built around a seed of love. When she sees you on top of the monkey bars in a place you know you are not allowed to be, she too walks over to where you are and instructs you to get down.

She then pulls you aside to talk with you, but what she says makes all the difference. She is going to approach this situation from a different perspective, a different understanding, and so she will use different words when she communicates with you.

She might say, "You know it's not acceptable for you to be on top of the monkey bars?" You might nod your head in response to that one.

Then she might say, "Do you understand why you are not allowed on the top of the monkey bars?" You might nod your head again.

She might elaborate and say, "You're not allowed on top of the monkey bars because it is not safe and it's our job to keep you guys safe when you're at school." That sounds like a pretty good reason, huh?

And as you stand there, she'll continue to talk to you. To walk you through what is going on. She might then say, "You understand that when you choose to break the rules, there are consequences to your actions?"

In her mind, she is not finding you at fault. Instead, she is following the simple premise of cause and effect. The cause is that you climbed on top of the monkey bars, something that you knew was not allowed.

She has already explained to you the effect or impact of your actions: that in breaking the rules you might sit alone or be sent to the principal's office.

When the context of the moment changes, the conversation itself changes, too. Rather than punishing you to teach you not to break the rules, the teacher holds you accountable for your actions.

Then it becomes an act of teaching. If you choose to become an endangerment to yourself and to others, a higher authority will need to step in to help you; to help mitigate potentially disastrous events. Who knows how many kids you inspired to climb on top of the monkey bars?

In this case, our second teacher is not trying to trigger shame or guilt within you. On the contrary, she's trying to help you understand, to redirect your behavior so it does not happen again. She does this in order to keep you safe, to keep other students safe (which is her job), and to teach you how to be a responsible human being who will grow up into a responsible adult. When you choose to break the rules, you will face repercussions meant to hold you accountable for the choices that you have made.

I would like you to take a moment to consider how you would respond to teacher #1 and teacher #2. Which teacher might earn your respect? From which teacher might you learn something more than class curriculum? Which teacher would you choose to go to for advice and aid in the future? In which situation would you have learned, in a healthy and loving way, not to climb on the monkey bars?

Sometimes we can fall into the trap of thinking that retribution or revenge is necessary to even the scales. But all retribution does is develop more problems. It creates a cycle in which the victim has been wounded and then the victim creates a problem by wounding the bully, increasing the pain in the world. Then, both individuals are victim and bully.

In this cycle we create a domino effect, where solving this conundrum requires more than one person changing their actions—it requires everyone involved to change their actions. And again, there comes this idea of community.

The teacher who acted with compassion without trying to trigger shame, guilt, or self-loathing still held that young you accountable, but did so in a way where it became a lesson and an opportunity to redirect your growth in a more healthy and productive manner. In order to become like teacher #2, you not only need a foundation wrapped around a seed of love; you also need to live with intention in the present moment.

When you live like teacher #2, you will have the foresight and the knowledge as you walk towards that student on the monkey bars to know what to say and how to go about saying it, to turn this moment into a lesson, a teachable moment, even if the student doesn't realize that's what's happening.

Which Seed Do You Choose?

Which sort of world do you wish to live in? How are you currently living your life?

Right now, most of the world is living their lives according to a Principle of Fear. As we've discussed and seen, our principle develops a specific kind of lifestyle, and therefore is directly linked with the quality of our human experience and the health of the Earth. Unfortunately, we can see evidence of fear everywhere:

- The news displays the worst moments and the greatest ills, not just locally but nationwide. The news stirs the pot of fear and drama and subliminally encourages people to relinquish control of their life for "protection and safety."

- The ads and commercials we are inundated with are designed based on an algorithm of need and worth. "You are unworthy, but if you buy X, all of your problems will be solved and you will be loveable." We know this to be a rotten apple, for you are lovable with your first breath.

- The polarization of different groups is meant to create division. Men vs. Women. Democrat vs. Republican. Straight vs. Gay. Rich vs. Poor. White vs. Black vs. Red vs. Yellow vs. Brown. Head vs. Heart.

- Shame, guilt, and fear are used by those in power to control the behavior of the masses. And through prolonged exposure, individuals begin to feel these emotions whenever they make a mistake.

- Society teaches us to reject certain traits, skills, desires, and dreams by openly ostracizing people who embrace these elements of their human selves. The result is that people find it hard to conceive of self-love when parts of themselves are rejected.

- Society teaches us to look for the person responsible. Who is to blame? How are they to be punished? These reactions are acts of fear and hatred based on fault, rather than of healing and growth based upon cause and effect.

All of these tools and cultural lifestyles are meant to create a divide in the people, to stop us from becoming the community that we are. It is from this place of fear that we are not only trained but indoctrinated to respond in a manner that creates and sustains pain and hardship. Fear creates a moment where self-judgment, hatred, and a need to survive are born.

But what comes of that? Do we learn? Do we grow? Does healing happen? Are we happy?

In the first scenario it becomes a battle, a war where it's about the person who comes out on top with more points. The second scenario is a life where we are a community, a village that supports one another, forgives one another, and accepts each other for the truth of who we are and the truth of what has happened in that moment.

For this reason, we must dump out our basket of apples and start at the very beginning. We must change how we understand life, what we recognize and accept as part of human nature, and what we recognize and accept as part of our society's nature.

It was from this place of understanding that I reached the conclusion that I wanted to build my life based on a Heart-Centered Lifestyle. I took that bedrock, or my basic understanding of the human experience, and personalized it with my seed of love.

The Head vs Heart Misunderstanding: A Rotten Apple

Recently, I uncovered a rotten apple within my personal philosophy: the belief that life is lived either from your head or your heart. Our society loves to polarize everything from politics to ethnicities to gender, and I have found that they have done the same thing with the idea of your head vs. your heart.

Here we see an apple: the idea that these two forces will always work in opposition with one another. This apple has been in my basket, and I have viewed and approached my life from this understanding. I had this apple before I knew about apples and the need to test them.

It wasn't until I was expanding my own knowledge that one of my teachers talked about the head and the heart working in tandem to guide you to new heights. This idea immediately clashed with the apple I carried.

When a new apple comes into conflict with an old apple, it means it's time to put some apples to the test. The first apple represents your own belief, and the second apple represents this new idea. Which one is wisdom? Which one is false wisdom? Which one(s) will I place into my new and improved basket?

What I discovered was that my understanding of the relationship between my head and my heart came from society's love of opposition—the old, "You're either with me or against me" idea, which is a literary fallacy.

So, if my understanding of my head and heart was built from false wisdom, maybe it is possible for my head to work with my heart. In sitting and giving this some thought, I found I agreed with my teacher's statement.

When I combine my head with my heart, I am not only able to live a life of love (as I wish to), but I can do so in a way where I remain wise, practical, and safe.

My head will caution me at times, suggesting practical ways to demonstrate my love. These ways will not only help keep me safe, but they will help me to take the emotion I carry within me and share it with the world.

Did you have the same false apple in your basket? Which apple(s) will you choose?

Chapter 2 Takeaways: Adding a Principle

- While the Ten Conclusions, provide the basics to human life and the bedrock for our personal philosophy, a principle provides us the personal touch that creates a lifestyle.
- A principle acts like a seed and will naturally nourish and promote various emotions and life experiences, depending on the type of principle.
- A Heart-Centered Principle naturally nourishes love, compassion, courage, strength, forgiveness, confidence, and so much more. A Heart-Centered Principle provides new tools, wisdom, and guidance to help us navigate and flourish in our life.

CHAPTER 3

Adding A Principle

I feel real
in this moment
I know pain
I know exhaustion
I know trauma
I know things that in my innocence
I didn't know before

in this moment I don't feel great
happiness and joy elude me

it is not a moment dreamed of
for who yearns for the aftermath of great pain?

but it's real
    I am no longer fighting what I feel
    not fighting what I think
    nor am I posturing for others

in this moment I am real
I am present in this moment
I am honoring each aspect

for this… I know pain is good
not because it is a happy experience
but because it is real

so I am too
and that's beautiful
that's a strange new wonderful

The darkness brought on by pain can blind us, causing our sight to desert us when we feel we need it most. In these instances, it can become easy to think that the world is cruel and harsh. When we experience pain or feel lost in this world, the truly debilitating element is not the pain but the ignorance. How do we heal? Where do we go? Where do we belong?

There are moments in my memory when I felt I traveled my life blindly. In these instances, I was tempted to stay where I was just as much as I was tempted to flee. We are so accustomed to knowing and being able to see the moving pieces of our lives that when we become blind, we can see ourselves as weak, wounded, or even abandoned. Yet, I have come to learn that sometimes what is best for us is to be blind.

In these instances, we must not only call on our courage but flip our perception upside down. It is only then that we can take our arms and reach out to the world. When we feel the desire to close in on ourselves, this is the moment to reach out and discover guidance. We must let our fingertips start the journey for us, grasping at what is available while our toes shift and carry us forward.

Oftentimes, it is not the wound that stops us—rather, it is our lack of knowledge on how to heal that prevents us from moving forward. The same is true about our purpose and place on Earth. The ignorance and blindness we experience is not the same as being stuck; it's just that we have been taught this false wisdom. We have been taught that anything less than perfect is flawed or even broken.

If you were born blind, you would not feel stuck or unable to move; rather, you would learn how to use your senses of touch and hearing to guide you. What stops you in your tracks is not the situation but your perception of the situation. If you see yourself as broken, un-lovable, un-savable, you will act as if you are. You will be the roadblock in your own healing.

As a child and even as an adult, there were moments when I felt stuck, blind to what to do or where I belonged. The pain was real in those moments, and if I had chosen to do nothing, that pain would still be inside me today.

Every person I have ever known has experienced pain. Yes, you could get into an argument about the trauma they sustained and how some individuals and even communities have had it harder than others, but what I have learned is that pain, no matter the source, still hurts. There's also no limit to the amount of pain in the world.

It's not about doling out pain to everyone in small doses. Instead, it's changing our lives, and our understanding of them, that will help us to reduce the amount of pain in the world. This idea then takes us right back to the roadblock called ignorance. How do we reduce pain?

Truthfully, there are a number of ways that we can reduce pain, and we've already started. When we took our understanding of life (our personal philosophy) and dumped out our basket of apples, we began the process of reducing pain.

By leaving rotten apples on the ground to decompose, we have left moments, thoughts, ideas, and policies that breed pain out of our basket and thus we have taken them out of our life. As a result, your life has less pain, the world has less pain. Now, we are taking another next step in our healing journey.

Faith and Love

As I sat down to write this book, I took many trips down memory lane to recall the fears, thoughts, and ideas I had back when I saw and lived my life from a place of fear. In the process, I recalled the great chasm in my understanding.

There were times when I felt that I stood on the edge of a cliff, unhappy about where I was, but unclear on how to get across to the other cliff where happiness was. In looking around me, I saw all these people living their own lives, and in the books I read, I kept discovering new worlds and adventures—proof that there was more to life.

This led me to think. Was my life what it was, or could I change it? Could I have a life like the ones I dreamed of? Could I end my pain and be happy?

Ultimately, it was a gem of self-love that pushed me into action. That, and my stubbornness. All in order to find out if life could be better. I didn't know what I was doing or where I was going, but I was unwilling to accept where I was.

I also remember hovering between my choices. I had encountered a moment in my life that required a leap of faith. An ambassador of fear had conjured an image where I failed and rather than traveling from where I was to the cliff across from me, where happiness lives, I fell. Fear did not want to let me go. It challenged me, and because of this it required me to have faith that I was moving onto a better world.

To better our lives, we need to make a change, because if our lives were working, we would be happy. I know that when we open ourselves up to this idea of change and entering into a better life, we also open the door to hope.

Hope on its own can seem out of place and even delusional, especially when thoughts based on fear run rampant in our mind. On account of this, we also need to embrace the faith that life can be better.

Who do you know or have seen with a life filled with happiness? What story have you read or seen that shows a human being living the type of life you desire? What proof have you witnessed that life can be better?

With that image in your mind, it's time to take that leap of faith where you join us in a happier world.

Your Worth and A Wounded Heart

There will come a day when children will be born into an environment where the traumas we have known will merely be cautionary tales in the history books. But I am not like the generations to come.

I built my life not with love, but with a seed of fear. During my life, I picked up some terrible habits, hurtful ideas, and debilitating philosophies. Due to this, I have experienced moments that didn't need to be painful but ended up so.

I also picked up a voice that sounds like me but is actually an ambassador of fear. A voice that calls on me to question my right to happiness and love.

As human beings, we categorize things, people included. We do this to understand, to control, and to get rid of unknown elements. But in doing so, we have created all sorts of twisted messages and ideas.

One damaging message is that people who have caused pain or have endured great pain are "broken." While this message is very common, it also is very debilitating, coming with all sorts of rotten truths.

Due to the pain we each have experienced, we can end up questioning what we deserve in life or even feeling that we won't ever be rid of our wounds. Because of this, I have found that there are some people who can't just rely on faith. They end up thinking, *"Just because there are those who live a better life, doesn't mean I will or get to."*

This idea can seem highly logical, but in actuality it's rotten in so many different ways. Not only does this statement neglect the Special Truth, but it also places a roadblock in our path—the idea that we won't ever be able to heal.

A Wounded Heart

Due to the strong presence of the Fear Principle, pain has touched each of us. As a result, we have been wounded. Unlike a paper cut that heals within days, some of our wounds are still with us—especially when we have yet to address them. Which has left many of us with wounded hearts.

When we have a wounded heart, we can acquire all sorts of silly ideas that lead us to question our worth and our right to a better life. Our wounded heart can even lead us to question our ability to achieve a thriving human experience.

So, we need to take a leap of faith, leaving behind what we know for a better world. We also need to introduce a new apple to our personal philosophy:

"I Am Worthy."

This apple is based on our Special Truth. When each person matters, our wellbeing matters. Even our pain matters, because we matter. When we apply this apple to our perception, we begin to see a bridge that will carry us across the cliff of fear and onto new land in a new and happy world.

Just like in the movie *Miracle on 34th Street* (1947), child Susan Walker (played by Natalie Wood) must take a leap of faith when she encounters the real Santa Claus. (Due to a rational mother, she does not believe in Santa.) Through the course of the movie, Santa asks her to believe. To achieve this, Susan Walker states over and over, "I believe, I believe…" in a tone that points out her disbelief. But by the end of the movie, she believes.

Faith and even our perceived self-worth acts in the same way as believing in Santa Claus. Sometimes, we must fake our faith or our own self-worth until we come to believe it in our hearts.

The Special Truth teaches us of our worth, but putting that worth into action can be difficult. Sometimes, we need to do the work that will lead us to happiness and treat ourselves as having worth, even if we don't completely believe it yet.

Through the process, we develop not only a perception of our worth and deeper faith in the good things in life, but we also develop a strong inner core. So, no matter who we encounter, no matter our history or our current environment, we believe that we are worthy, and so we can walk across the bridge to a brighter world.

MESSAGES FROM SPIRIT AND THE UNIVERSE

During the course of my own journey, I was sent signs that I was not only on the right path but making great headway. One of these signs was a small bear cub that ran across the road in the middle of the day. We receive these messages from Spirit to remind us that we never walk alone.

When we combine the knowledge that Spirit is loving and that we are special, we discover that we not only have the right but the ability to ask for assistance. Even when there are no other people around us, it does not mean we have been deserted. Even when we are blind to the path before us, it doesn't mean we have been abandoned.

As you continue to take this healing journey, I encourage you to call on Spirit and your spirit guides to help let you know that you are on the right path. Why take a harder journey than you need to? Instead, why not lighten your load by accepting the help they are waiting to offer you?

The House Analogy: The Process of Healing

I have a heart that has not only been wounded but has healed. I am taking a healing journey that will not only help me recuperate from wounds I have sustained but build a life where I limit the pain I will experience moving forward.

Yet due to my wounded heart, I am not starting from scratch and building a sweet basket of apples. I am bringing with me into this moment some rotten apples.

While I would have loved building my castle of dreams from scratch, I didn't catch on about personal philosophies and perceptions until I already had a personal philosophy of my own. Just as building a home from scratch with all the latest technologies would be wonderful, remodeling is its own kind of complicated.

This past year, my mother and I completed the remodeling of the home we now live in. Due to the Covid-19 pandemic, we were both there to witness our contractor take apart and put back together our home. At that same time, I was attempting to complete Volume One and was able to draw parallels between healing and remodeling. That's why I liken our healing process with the remodeling process.

The House Analogy

Imagine yourself as a home. Within the four outer walls there are different rooms for different parts of yourself and the décor acts as a reflection of who you are. This home has the potential to be a castle of your dreams, but is currently in need of renovations to remove the toxins and missing support beams.

Since you already have a personal philosophy in place and we are not creating a healthy understanding of life with our first breath, we need to remodel what we already have. Due to this scenario, the path we take will be different than what a contractor would do for a brand-new home.

The Foundation

In Volume One, I explained the importance of our personal philosophy, and how our Ten Conclusions will create the bedrock for our new life. In starting at the beginning, we were able to take the cracked foundation of our home and heal the very space in which our house will sit.

The House

The outer walls of our home are comprised of our new principle. This seed of love will touch each element of our lives and surround us in a new world and a new way of living, protecting us from the outside world and supporting us from within.

Our next step is to address each room within our house and make the changes that we need to not only have a healthy and safe space but also to enjoy the room. Turning our house into the personalized home of our dreams.

The process of working on the house will bring with it dust, dirt, noise, and a shuffling of things as we decide how we will honor the kitchen (home-life), bedroom (self), office (work), family room (family), as well as the other rooms. Our healing process acts in a similar manner as to what I experienced during our remodeling.

We need to decide what will do with each room.
- What changes do we need to make for safety reasons?
  - Do we need to make changes to our perception in order to see things in a healthy manner? We can achieve this by taking the time to utilize our Ten Conclusions and applying them to how we see and understand the various elements of our life.

- What will be the purpose of the room?
  - We must choose to honor each part of ourselves—our self, family, friends, work, and our fun and serious sides.

- What sort of changes or compromises will you need to make?
  - Sometimes our past trauma influences what is possible for us moving forward. While we are on a healing journey, we still will carry with us all we have been. We are marked by our life, both the positive and negative experiences. Therefore, we are not always able to fulfill this pristine image within our mind.

    As we heal, we do not return to the past, but move forward. This forward momentum takes us away from a state of survival and pain and into a life of harmony. That is the end result that we cultivate by healing and changing our lives. But in doing so, we do not erase the past.

    Throughout this healing journey, who you will become is a result of your choices and your past. You might experience physical or mental limitations due to past life experiences that will lead you to change your plans. But these changes do not have to be negative or disheartening. They hold the potential to lead you to a life you never imagined for yourself, one that holds love and happiness as a result of your healing.

- How will we honor our unique selves?
  - Like our Heart-Centered Principle, what are some apples and choices that we can make to honor who we are and what we like? How can we personalize our philosophy and life to honor and reflect who we are?

- Purging our things.
  - Are there some rotten apples we need to leave on the ground?

- Getting new and needed items.
    - Do we need some new ideas or tools in place of some of those rotten apples? Do we need new ideas or tools in order to create new life experiences we've been dreaming of?

Just like in remodeling a house, there is only so much work that can be accomplished within a single day. There are also times when a certain room of our life needs more of our attention than another.

Each day or moment we spend addressing the different areas of our lives leads us to a deeper level of healing. Each time I return to my philosophies and to my way of life, I pull back the layers and achieve a more well-rounded and complete level of healing. Thus, I've reduced the amount of fear and pain in my life.

I know in a world of instant gratification this idea might seem strange, but some things just take time. Whether it's renovating a house and turning it into a home, or taking a healing journey, time and hard work provide each of us the chance to live a prosperous life.

Fear and the Brain

When I think back to the times when I've been confused and in pain, the emotions I know I experienced are missing from my memories. I can spend my days happy and content, but I also know the lull and influence that fear had over me. I'm all too familiar with that voice that tries to convince you of its lies.

But the thing I've learned about living your life in fear is that you never stop. Even when you reach a safe place or have enough food, skills, funds, tools, or support, you still operate from this place of survival. You end up never knowing what it's like to thrive.

This fear-based perception will trap us until we choose to switch our chosen seed.

We see evidence of fear's influence in our lives when we take a look at the fight-or-flight response. In 1915, Walter Bradford Cannon referred to the "necessities of fighting or flight" in the first edition of *Bodily Changes in Pain, Hunger, Fear and Rage*. Since that time, science has broken down the fight-or-flight response on a physiological level.

While the reaction that we experience causes physiological changes, the triggering element is psychological fear. When a dog growls or a car honks, we each experience a unique response depending on how we perceive the experience.

For those who perceive the dog growling or the car honking as something that could endanger their lives, their perception triggers a response on a basic survival level. In response to this perceived threat, the brain sends a bunch of signals that triggers changes within our body.

If you think of a time when you experienced a perceived threat, you'll remember how your heart started racing, adrenaline rushed through your blood stream, and your senses seemed to strengthen. All of these physiological responses are meant to prepare you for what's to come so that you stay alive.

While this flight, fight, or freeze state can't be controlled, the triggering element *can* be. Since it is our psychological fears that trigger this response, our perception of life influences how often we experience this stress response.

Yes, there are some situations in life that endanger our well-being and having a fight-or-flight response just might save us, but other situations in life don't need to be seen with fear. If we live our lives based on fear, we increase the number of situations to fear in this world. Consequently, we experience an increased amount of stress. But we can change this simply by altering how we choose to approach our life. By selecting a Heart-Centered Lifestyle, we reduce and eliminate fearful moments from our present as well as from our future.

The Gift of Deep Breathing

Within a world still healing, there are things we must fear if we wish to live. We can have a wounded heart and sometimes, we can become wounded due to trauma. Trauma can then create an overactive state that excessively triggers our fight-or-flight response. Whether we've experienced trauma or not, there are times when we will experience stress of varying levels.

However, this doesn't mean that we need to accept this stress and fear in our lives. We can utilize tools to cope, such as relaxation techniques, regular exercise, and social support. One such relaxation technique is deep breathing.

While we work to change our perception, to stop seeing life from a fearful place, we can also utilize deep breathing to change our brain waves. Which will change the moment we are experiencing from one of length to a short moment of anxiety and stress.

We experience five different types of brain waves ranging from an excited state to deep and utter relaxation, (Gamma, Beta, Alpha, Theta, and Delta). When we take time to breathe deeply, we can influence our brain waves and our stress levels. In the study titled *Study of Brain Activity Analysis of Deep Breathing* conducted at Mae Fa Luang University in Thailand by Wanee Rojviroj, Professor Dr. Vichit Punyahotra, Assistant Professor Dr. Wichian Sittiprapaporn, and Dr. Ariya Sarikaphuti, they, discovered that deep breathing induced relaxation and improved mental health.

Due to the impact deep breathing has on brainwaves, test subjects were successful in experiencing an Alpha brainwave. Alpha brainwaves are where we not only experience our body and mind in a relaxed state but a clear mind and a boost in creativity. So, not only can we connect with the world by breathing deeply, but we can improve the quality of our mental state.

Fear Transference

I have striven to reduce and remove unnecessary fear from my life and replace it with faith, love, and healthy tools. Yet, as I have worked towards change, fear hasn't wanted to leave and has made a point of tagging along. Throughout this process, fear has led me to question the efficacy and abilities of my new way of life.

I believe that we are so accustomed to a certain state of being that the habit paired with the nature of fear can leave us open to confusion. Maybe we don't feel rational, reasonable, or safe with a life of love. This can be due to the fact that we have mis-identified fear as rationalism or practicality.

When we heal from fear, we can feel that we're placing too much on faith. Our life and our decisions can become devoid of common sense. When fear dominates our decisions and our actions; we can become so accustomed to a state of fear that to be without it boggles the mind. When we heal from fear, we can be left confused about which way is up.

During the beginning of the Covid-19 pandemic, the media released a photo of people lined up to get into the grocery store in the background, with a grocery cart filled with toilet paper in the foreground. This photo was a message meant to justify and stimulate fear in the masses in order to regulate and control the people. Here, we see a society of fear not wanting to let us go. It then becomes even more challenging to release fear from our lives.

Whatever the case may be, we can end up placing fear into our new practices, beliefs, tools, and philosophes—not because these practices are weak, but because we are used to feeling worried, concerned, and afraid.

For example, in Volume One, we learned about energy and of the Six Safety Tools we can utilize to help keep us safe. This knowledge helps us understand the nature of life and our interconnectedness. It also empowers us as we discover different ways that we can improve the quality of our lives.

However, if we aren't attentive, we can end up opening the door to fear and weaving unnecessary concern into our new and at one time healthy knowledge and tools. Then, all of a sudden, energy is no longer an empowering truth but an opening in our lives for concern and fear to enter.

As we begin to shift our lives to a more self-aware, spiritual, and Heart-Centered style, it can become easy to take that fear with us and weave it into the fabric of our beings. So, what do we do? How do we leave fear in our rearview mirror and transform our life into one of love?

With such a tough question it's easy to fall back on our road map, the rulebook that has guided us all our life. But it's precisely your rule book, your personal philosophy, that we're rebuilding. Your personal philosophy comes with a nice big helping of fear—that's why we can fall into the trap of fear transference.

It is the human factor, it is us, that brings fear. To eradicate and heal from fear, we must learn to become present in the moment. Rather than seeing the world based on fear, we can approach our life from the knowledge that we are safe, that our lives is a gift from a loving, guiding, and supportive creator (Conclusion #5).

We know deep within our being that we are protected and in a place where you can thrive and enjoy wonderful connections with wonderful people in a wonderfully beautiful environment.

Opening Back Up

A wounded heart is like any wound: it is through putting our body and heart back out there that we not only heal but continue to thrive. If we were to break our arm, we would give ourselves time to heal, and then we would start building back our strength. We might even attempt to rush the healing process, eager to get back to the dexterity we once knew. The same is true with a wounded heart.

If you were to break your arm, you wouldn't say, "I'm never going to use my arm again!" Can you image trying to live your life with only one arm or one leg when you have two?

So why have we created a culture where we say, "I'm never going to love again!" or, "I'm going to die all alone!"? Despite our trauma and pain, we still have a heart. So why wouldn't we use it?

Just like a broken bone, it is important that after we sustain an injury to our heart, we give ourselves time to heal. Time to rebuild our strength and learn some new tools. After we do, it's time to open ourselves back up. To take a chance again and connect with those we know as well as strangers.

Without our hearts, we won't be able to live Heart-Centered Lives. If we choose to never again use our hearts, we not only numb our pain but the emotions of love and happiness as well. As you travel on this healing journey, give yourself time to heal. Then, when you're ready, or maybe feel "almost" ready, open up. Start small and grow. Test your limits as you would test your arm's strength and reach back out to the world. Live a full and thriving life.

Chapter Three Takeaways: The Wounded Heart

- Since we began our life with a seed of fear, we have wounded hearts.
- These wounded hearts mean that we not only need to learn new tools for a new and healthy life, but we must also unlearn the coping mechanisms of our youth.
- To achieve this transformation, we need to take a leap of faith while also living our lives from this place of worth, even if we don't believe just yet.
- When we live our lives based on fear, we will forever be stuck in a state of fear.
- As our wounded hearts heal, there will come a time when we must open back up in order to reconnect with the world and afford ourselves the opportunity to live a thriving life once more.

CHAPTER 4

Authentic Love

we dance a while, we paint
we find time to embrace
we smile and we laugh
we sway in time with space

but within our hearts
we seem to wait
waiting for something
yet to take place

for some
they wait to feel safe
for happiness, love
maybe even fate

we wait
    and wait
and seem to get
is such a despondent state

we travel this path
well-worn and beaten
the lines are clear and even

but what if our parents are wrong
what if what we've been waiting for
has been here all along

what if within life's dance
hidden beneath layers
of painted masks

lies our desire, a reality buried
by our own two hands

what if instead we removed
the layers of deception
spent our time living,
not counting down the hours

how much might we thrive?

When we began our healing journey, we started in the world of philosophy. We took a practical, up-front approach to the nature of reality. From this practical consideration, we created the Ten Conclusions that act as our bedrock.

The next step was to add a seed, a way that we wish to live our lives. In doing so we've entered into a vague world of emotions. We utilized the word, an idea of "fear" and "love." Yet we can sometimes utilize words without understanding their full meaning.

What does love mean? What does it look like? What does it feel like? How does this word translate into a way of life?

I realized as I was putting together this second volume that I was falling into a trap. I was assuming that you, the reader, would know what love is. I then had a conversation with a friend who told me he couldn't remember the last time he'd been happy. He couldn't use that memory to help push him to improve his life and empower him when he felt powerless.

How do I know you know what it's like to love or to feel love?

So, take a moment and avoid this assumption trap with me. Don't require yourself to know something that you've never been exposed to. Rather than assuming you know about it, let's talk about love.

What is Love?

Love is a choice. It is an emotion that can be described as gentle and soothing, supportive and protective, as well as fiery and all encompassing. What makes love and sadly even fear such a great seed for our lives is that they know such a huge breadth.

Love has the capacity to still our being and influence our actions and words not only in the gentle and supportive moments, but in the fiery and impassioned ones as well. Love not only provides us a wonderful way to live our lives, but is capable of traversing every aspect of our lives and becoming a useful navigator.

One way we can see love's ability to stretch is in the way that it becomes a building block for other wonderful emotions and tools in our lives. Love gives birth to compassion, forgiveness, patience, courage, vitality, creativity, empowerment, and so many other wonderful components. In this way, love colors our lives.

It provides us the skills to nurture our own selves and thus enter a Heart-Centered Life. While there are many components to understanding love—after all, it is capable of filling every nook and cranny of our lives— this is a wonderful place to start.

What Kind of Love?

With love's capacity to meld with other emotions and develop strengths like compassion and courage, it is time to consider just what type of love we are seeking. For love can also meld with the emotion of fear and create unhealthy and toxic patterns. When we consider a Heart-Centered Life, we don't want it to be an amalgamation of love and fear. Rather, we want to utilize a healthy love.

With this healthy love, we want to embrace every component and aspect of ourselves, others, and the world around us. This is why we need an authentic love, and we need to understand just what that means.

An Authentic Love

Firstly, love is a choice, a willingness to open our hearts and embrace it. The second component to an authentic love is authenticity. To achieve this authenticity, we must accept the truth:
- Of who we are.
- Of who others are.
- Of where we are in our life's journey.

It's easy to love someone or something when we see the positive, when we see the finished product, or even when we identify with others as being like us. But love becomes authentic, a Heart-Centered Life, when we can see the differences, the mistakes, the wounds, the trauma sustained and the trauma inflicted. It becomes an authentic love when we know both the light and the darkness within another person, as well as within ourselves.

For Example

A simple but I think a telling example of an authentic love can be found in the way in which I view and treated my kittens, Thomas and Oliver. As kittens, they loved to engage with each other and play, but their human family (my mom and me) were still not safe from their claws or teeth.

A fear-based principle would have a person become enraged and angered when the kitten mistakes them for another kitten to play with. But an authentic love will utilize the truth: that cats and kittens are still animals. That they have claws and teeth and when they are young, they do not realize that people are not cats.

When we accept this truth, our actions and reactions play out differently. Rather than being the angry person, you can carefully disengage with the kitten, redirect their behavior, and turn a scratch or a bite into a teachable moment.

While this is a simple example, it shows how a single moment of your life can be lived without anger and without fear. The moment when the kittens attacked my body lasted a shorter amount of time when I chose to create a teachable moment. Due to my choice, the moment of danger and destruction (tiny claws and teeth can inflict a lot of damage) passed quickly because it wasn't filled with anger and resentment.

When the moment passes, you have the opportunity in the next moment for a hug or to tend to yourself and experience a moment of love—authentic love for your kittens, and love for yourself as seen by taking the time to tend to your wounds.

But as I've been saying, in order to experience love and utilize it to create teachable moments, redirect behavior, and be part of the solution, you need to be present in the moment. If you're lost in thought or your mind and heart are engaged in the past or in the future, then you are not in a place where you are capable of stepping back and seeing the situation for what it is, nor are you capable of accepting it as it is.

When you're not present, you are not in a place to redirect a reaction from one of anger to one of love. But when you respond consciously and mindfully, you can remove unnecessary anger and trauma from your own life. Authentic love means that we know the truth of ourselves and of others, of a scenario or experience we're having.

Facades: The Masks We Wear and Make

We create masks, false personas for ourselves and for others, and because of them, we know pain. We come to know heartbreak. When we look into the mirror or at the people around us, we see, know, and approach a given situation through the eyes of these masks.

A mask acts as a wall, a divide between ourselves and others. This wall blocks connections, blocks true love, authentic love— the very thing we are seeking.

We enter into situations with these preconceived notions about how they will go, how others will react, how we or they will feel and think, but most importantly, we enter these moments with masks donned and in hand. I myself have been guilty of seeing both myself and others through the eyes of a mask.

Personal Masks

As for myself, I have been known to wear a mask when I gaze into the mirror. When I do, I create a block between me and my true self, cutting myself off from my own love and support.

For many, when we look into the mirror, we oftentimes choose what we see. We tell ourselves a story that is composed of the parts we know and wish to be, or parts that have been created by others. As such, we can see all sorts of strange things looking back at us.

We can be the perfect creation who doesn't have any problems, our mask blinding us to our imperfections, our wounds, and the vulnerability we wish not to see. Here, we can see the ego and pride in control.

On the other hand, we can gaze into the mirror and see only our faults: a damaged person unworthy of love, and even sometimes unworthy of life. The voice of fear points out all of our flaws. Our insecurities seem larger than life. But these are not truths that we see reflected back at us. Rather, they are masks constructed by half-truths, and they greatly endanger us. They divide us from the very thing that we seek: love.

With these masks, so much damage is done:
- We restrict our own love.
- We justify our actions and opinions.
- We justify denying love from others.
- We block ourselves from love.
- We never truly see ourselves.

As such, we aren't in a place to build a connection with ourselves or others, or to heal.

We also invent scenarios and environments that create blocks between ourselves and others. We feel others never truly loved us because they didn't ever know us, mostly because they never saw anything but the masks we chose to wear. Then comes the danger of what we do to other people.

Masks for Others

We often look at others through the masks we give them. These masks are created by our dreams and desires, our fears, or our limited understanding of other people. Then, when we interact with them, all sorts of problems arise.

We become disenchanted or disappointed when they fail to live up to our dreams. They never feel loved or honored, because we fail to see them behind the masks we have given them.

Between the masks we wear, the ones we create for others, the masks they wear, and the ones they create for us, we form a chasm of four layers that divides and blocks us from the very things we seek: love, acceptance, truth, and compassion.

To truly embark on a life based on love, we must:
- See ourselves.
- Know ourselves.
- Develop the confidence to show ourselves to others.
- Be open-minded to the truth of others.
- Grant ourselves and others time to know and to figure life out.
- Be patient with ourselves and others.
- Be accepting of the human capacity for making mistakes and having faults.

All while decluttering from the falsehoods of before.

While this long list of steps towards authentic love can seem huge and even impossible, at the end of the day, how we go about learning about ourselves and others follows the same method. Accepting others and ourselves for who we are is the same act, and when we learn the tools, the process of accepting and being open becomes part of our subconscious skill set. It becomes the new manner in which we live, as natural to us as breathing.

Accept the Non-Answer

Through time, wounds, and even growth, we can lose our sense of self. Who you are changes as you grow from a child to an adult. If we fail to remain connected with ourselves, we can become disconnected from who we are and who we have become.

As we heal and reconnect, we can choose to follow the path developed by society, or a more holistic path. You don't need self-imposed or societal-imposed certainty, but you do need a place that helps you to transform those moments when you become lost.

I think back to all the times I was in doubt, when I lost my connection with myself, my beliefs, even my connection with others, when I did not have the answers. I didn't know how to get to that place where I wasn't lost anymore. That portion of my life's journey could have been much harder than it needed to be, and it was already challenging.

The people and community that we choose can act as a light, guiding us out of the darkness that is ignorance and disconnection. For we don't need to find our way alone. I cannot express the level of appreciation I have for my mother, who has chosen to support me throughout each stage of my healing journey. Whether that has been to give me space to work things out internally or help remind me of my worth with that special magical power moms seem to possess.

We can also elevate our experience by not pushing or rushing ourselves to have the answers to who we are, how quickly we arrive, or what will become of us. In addition to choosing people who will provide us the space we need and not rush us in our journey.

For each time I became lost, I found within the darkness a deeper understanding and love for myself. By being lost, we enter a stage in our journey where lacking the answers is the correct response. By acknowledging that we don't know, we open up a space within ourselves for an answer, which, with time, will present itself and lead us once more into the sunlight.

As we enter the sunlight, we are changed, for more of our selves has been brought with us. We become more authentic, and understand and love ourselves to a greater degree. These are healing journeys if we treat them as such.

The last component of living a Heart-Centered Life is the truth of transformation. When we choose to love the truth of things, that love will change and transform overtime. This shift occurs because the truth of who we are and how we understand life changes and grows as we do.

Chapter Four Takeaways: Authentic Love

- To avoid the assumption fallacy, it is important that we don't hold ourselves to the standard of knowing something we have never been exposed to, like love.
- In living a Heart-Centered Life, we don't just want love, but a healthy and authentic love.
- To achieve this type of love, we need to stop wearing masks and facades, and we need to stop applying them to other people. This is the only way we can achieve the connection and authenticity that we are seeking.
- Sometimes we don't have an answer, and by accepting this, we open and create space inside of ourselves to be filled by the answer when it presents itself. This approach is a more holistic and kinder manner befitting our Heart-Centered Lifestyle.

CHAPTER 5

Understanding Love

crisp and bright
it curls and forms
a thing of beauty

ruby velvet caresses the
sun that shines upon its face

with the dawn it curls
full beads, glistening wet

as time passes
age sets in
and wrinkles form

yet its thorns remain
beauty and strength
even in age

Now that we have a basic understanding about the love we are seeking, our next step is to learn a little bit more about the different qualities and textures of love.

To live a Heart-Centered Lifestyle means choosing to love not only ourselves and our friends and family, but people and the world. In order to understand just how that will work, we're going take a look at the two styles and ten categories of love.

Unconditional Love

When we choose to live a life of love, we choose to love strangers and the planet. This is our unconditional love. We do not require anything of the outside world, and we accept people and the world for exactly who they are. We embrace their light and their darkness. We choose to not place any masks in the way of these connections.

But how do we do this and still remain healthy, happy, and safe?

We utilize a spoon.

When I sat down to consider what a life of love looks like, I realized that my first response will mimic my life of fear. My first response will be born of love, just as it was once born of fear. Unconditional love will be about loving everything I see and everyone I meet.

While we continue to improve the quality of life and our connections as a community, we share unconditional love. We accept people, society, and life as they are. Acknowledging that there is still healing and change that we need, hence why this love is unconditional.

This unconditional love creates an environment that naturally supports and gives birth to a world of love, healing, happiness, and positive transformation. It removes the need for revenge, prejudice, unworthiness, and conflict. Not only does unconditional love help to trigger a transformation to the nature of life and the world we live in, but it also positively impacts our personal lives.

But as I began envisioning my love as I doled it out, I felt overwhelmed and drained. My heart is only so big and holds only so much love. So how do I still love my family and friends, and love the rest of the world? How do I love the universe, too? This panic (old fear seed showing up) led me to my spoonful analogy.

The Spoonful Analogy

Imagine your heart as a vessel. Inside this vessel we hold all the love we possess. When we have moments of connection with the world, we dip into our hearts and share our love.

How do we know how much to share?

We utilize a spoon.

With each connection, we dip into our hearts and share a spoonful. When we connect with those whom we consider family and friends, we share two spoonfuls, and when we love ourselves, we share three-plus spoonfuls. This is how we live a Heart-Centered Life: sharing our love with everyone and still remaining healthy. (Head + Heart)

You might start out with a very small spoon. This might mean that as you encounter the outside world, you merely share common courtesy (basic human kindness).

As you heal, learn, and experience some challenging moments in your life, your heart will grow. Your capacity for love will grow, and so too will the size of your spoon.

As your love grows, you might be able to not only be polite to others, but offer a listening ear, a piece of advice, or invite someone to jump ahead of you at the grocery store when they only have a few items to your many. All of these are ways to support the community we share without conditions, and without endangering yourself. You're not taking on someone else's problem, nor are you getting overly emotionally attached, but you are still spreading the love.

Can you think of a time when a stranger helped you out when they didn't need to?

Can you remember a time when someone was unnecessarily aggressive or horrible?

What was your response in each instance? If you got to choose, which experience would you have more often: one of kindness or one of aggression?

How can you share love with the world?
How big is your spoonful today?
How big was your spoon five years ago?

Through the use of our Spoonful Analogy, we not only achieve a Heart-Centered lifestyle, but learn how to share the love that we possess in an unconditional and safe manner.

Conditional Love

When we choose to approach our lives from a place of love, this integral component of our personal philosophy will influence every aspect of our being. We can then take what we know about love and combine it with other wisdom to uncover more about the nature of life. This process will not only strengthen and alter your perception, but it will also provide you with new tools and wisdom.

With love as an integral component of our lives, we can see how the different categories of love manifest different textures. When we live a life of love, we know that with each experience comes the potential for love. This is how we experience a life of happiness, healing, love, compassion, courage, and all those other wonderful emotions. In viewing the world through a lens of love and more specifically self-love, we manifest the style of conditional love.

As we saw with unconditional love, this new layer to our perception takes our understanding of authentic love and applies it to every facet of the external world. We add an additional layer when we introduce conditional love to our lives.

This is when we begin to see the textures that come with a prosperous life. These diverse and multi-layering of love enrich our human experience.

In choosing to love the world, we change the nature of our lives, and we utilize the influence we have in life to change the world itself. We change what the human experience means on a global scale.

But when it comes to our personal lives, we must acknowledge that not everybody is in a healthy place. Some people are still, intentionally and unintentionally, bringing great pain into the world.

When we choose to live a Heart-Centered Life utilizing authentic love, we not only love the external world and all we encounter, but we choose to love ourselves.

To uncover what conditional love is, we must take a moment to consider what self-love looks like. From the simple fact that we love ourselves, we learn that the decisions we make, our understanding of ourselves, the world around us, and so much more will shift. This shift will influence our words and actions, thus, we will manifest a different life.

We also learn that our safety and happiness become an important and integral deciding factor in our lives. So, if we are meant to ensure our safety and happiness in a thriving life, then we must make decisions that reflect this goal and thus will lead us to that end result we desire.

When we combine the two truths of what it means to love ourselves and the fact that there are still lost and wounded souls in the world, then we learn that we must become selective in who we choose to become part of our inner circle. This personal environment is our sanctuary on Earth, and it will only remain a sanctuary if healthy people are part of it.

Conditional love then becomes the manner in which we choose our inner circle. We select people in communities and organizations that reflect the ideals and values that we have. Thus, we create a support system for the people who join our community, as well as for ourselves.

We define this style of love as conditional because we have standards that we utilize to select who we choose as friends and who we choose as family. I would like to note that these conditions reflect who we are as people.

As human beings, we make mistakes. When you consider the qualities you need from the people you allow into your sanctuary, consider what you can give:

- Try hard to do well and be kind.
- Display compassion when mistakes are made.
- Work to communicate so neither of you are in the dark.
- Honor the Golden Rule and be considerate.

Not only will these requirements help you select people for your sanctuary, but they are also wonderful qualities to demonstrate to others. As you invite these people into your life, they will be doing the same. You then become the external world for them, and how you act and what you say will determine if they are safe inviting you into their sanctuary.

So, consider what you need and desire from others, and what you have to offer. From these questions you can shape a list of requirements and desires for the people who you will invite deep within your heart.

BRAVING

Another marvelous tool comes from research storyteller Brené Brown, Ph.D., LMSW. Her work in shame and vulnerability has unearthed new wisdom and the strength of these new truths has the ability to shake up our very understanding.

In her Super Soul Session, *The Anatomy of Trust*, Brené Brown breaks down the various elements to trust.

Here's a brief overview of her groundbreaking acronym. **We can not only utilize this tool to help improve our communication with others, but we can also use BRAVING to help guide us to people that will fit into our inner circle.** For a more in-depth look at BRAVING and how we can use it in our life, I highly recommend you check out her website (www.brenebrown.com) to see what the expert has to say.

B – Boundaries
R – Reliability
A – Accountability
V – Vault: (We display confidentiality, not sharing what others have shared with us and trusting that others will keep what we have shared private.)
I – Integrity
N – Non-judgement
G – Generosity

My final recommendation is to be open. Having too many requirements is very similar to demanding perfection, and you never know who might make a wonderful addition to your life. Some of my best friends were not the people with whom I had an obvious connection, but the people who invested their time to get to know me, share who they were, and were respectful of my own beliefs and person. So, be open, because the shape and size of a person might be different than you imagined but exactly what you needed.

I'd also like to note that just because you don't connect with someone on a deep enough level to invite them into your inner circle doesn't change the truth of unconditional love. While they may not be a friend or family member, they are still human beings.

By adopting these two styles of love, we begin building a well-rounded, Heart-Centered Life. Designed to honor every facet of not only our human experience but life itself.

The Ten Categories

Love. With this single word we paint a picture. We identify the things that we feel kinship towards. We identify the things that hold value for us, and yet the word love itself means a great many things.

I love my family and I love dark chocolate. But the quantity and style of my love are two different things. With a single word we paint a picture.

As we've seen, love offers a richness and texture that elevates our lives. Yet understanding this broad emotion can be difficult, especially when we only use the word "love." Which is why I have studied various cultures, psychologists, and philosophers, and their understanding of the word "love." In pursuit of my own development, my research has led me to the ancient Greeks.

Not only do the ancient Greeks offer wise philosophers who have taught me a thing or two about the nature of reality, they also offer ten different categories, or ten different textures, to love.

From these ten different categories we can begin to understand the depth and breadth that love offers us in life. With that in mind, we can better understand the very seed that we have chosen to utilize as we approach our life from this new healing place.

As I have researched these terms, I have found an inconsistency in order and number. For this reason, I have placed these ten categories into an order of my choosing, starting first with the love most of us experienced at birth.

Agape: Unconditional Love

We experienced this boundless compassion and infinite empathy when we were first born. As our parent(s) and family held us, they did so with love. We didn't need to speak, do, or be anything or anyone in order to receive this love.

In Volume One, I encouraged you to start loving yourself before we even began our work. To love yourself with your first breath, just like when you were a child.

Take a moment to consider the texture and quality of this love. When have you experienced unconditional love? What does *agape*, or unconditional love, mean to you?

Consider your parents (biological or chosen) as they held you. They chose to love you before you ever did anything. You weren't perfect nor free of mistakes. You hadn't achieved great success. You were just you, and you were loved.

Agape is a love free of any desires, expectations, wants, needs or standards, and for a lot of people, it's known as the divine truth. Many people have discovered through their understanding of Spirit that Spirit loves us unconditionally.

Consider the strength of this love, its inability to be broken. If you aren't required to do or say anything to be loved, then no matter the mistakes, you are still embraced.

Influence of Fear on *Agape*

As I considered the texture of unconditional love, I couldn't help but think about how foreign this love is. In looking around me, in reflecting on my society and culture, I realized that nowhere was I taught to love unconditionally.

Yes, I was taught to love, but I was taught to love family because of genetics, friends because of companionship, and eventually lovers because of worth, status, and prospects. None of the relationships that society taught me about had anything to do with unconditional love. Yet, it is the most unbreakable form of love there is.

When others wish to control people, disempower, and harm them, they introduce fear into the relationship. A fear seed influences a society to neglect this texture of love. And sadly, if we never question what we were taught, we may have never noticed that this love was missing from our lives. Did you even know that you could love without conditions? That you are loved unconditionally by Spirit?

Philautia: Self-Love

As I write these words, the concept of self-love still remains one of the most neglected textures to love. Yet, self-love is needed in order for us to not only care for ourselves, but to care for others.

For how can we share an emotion if we are foreigners to it? What I mean by this is that you cannot share what you don't know, have, or understand. How can we demonstrate a healthy love for others if we deny it to ourselves?

In Buddhist philosophy, philautia is known as self-compassion—the concept being that self-love gentles our approach to our own selves. As we travel on our healing journey and live our human experience, we will encounter moments where what we see isn't nice or right.

With the mistakes we've made in the past, and the strong likelihood of mistakes that we'll make in the future, self-love acts as a means of stepping back and analyzing so we may learn and heal in a healthy and compassionate manner.

We saw another manifestation of self-love when we encountered conditional love. Here, self-love helps us to remain safe and balanced in our lives. When we love ourselves, we take the time to consider who we want around us. Not only does self-love aid us in seeing the entirety of ourselves (both the light and the darkness), but it provides a plethora of other textures to our lives.

Self-love, while one of the most critical components to life, can be one of the most elusive forms of love in a society where self-judgment and shame are critical components. Therefore, self-love takes time and a greater understanding to put into action. But don't worry, we will be addressing philautia more deeply within this volume later on.

Storge: Familial Love

While self-love can be elusive, storge is oftentimes the next love we consciously know. As children, we embrace ourselves because we follow the example of our family.

We briefly touched upon family when we took a look at conditional love. Now I'd like you to take a moment to think about how you define family, and then compare this understanding to what the Ancient Greeks have to say.

Familial love not only refers to those to whom we are related, but to the connections we experience in our youth. Just as we cried out and wiggled to see how the world responded, the bonds we created in childhood were the first instances of human connection that we experienced. As a result, they were the first examples and first teachers we had about family, love, and the ways of the world.

We created these bonds before we knew heartbreak, before our rational, adult minds stepped in to protect us or attempt to protect us. These bonds have then shaped our perspectives influencing our present day and future relationships.

There are two elements to familial love, according to the ancient Greeks. The first aspect of familial love focuses on those to whom we are related. This type of family holds importance, not necessarily on a love level, but in a primitive, we-must-survive kind of level. The bonds have created a way for us to define community. They are also a way for us to survive, so that we, as young, are taken care of, and when we age, as elders, we are again taken care of. Family in this sense brings with it obligation and sometimes even an absence of choice.

Because we can feel disconnected from our families, we can sometimes experience a sense of disempowerment if our families are not who we need them to be. Just because you are related to someone does not mean that you connect with them, and just because someone holds the position of parent doesn't mean they are kind or safe. Due to these truths I encourage you to question how you handle your familial obligations.

In the absence of obligation, maintaining familial ties becomes a choice. We are empowered with free-will, and in choosing to keep our family close it increases the quality of love we share with them. When we see family as a choice, the love we experience is not borne out of obligation but comes from an actual, authentic place of admiration and appreciation.

And for those who have experienced a toxic environment, the power of choice allows you to say "no," to walk away, to create boundaries, and to advocate for your needs. When we embrace the power of choice, we discover that we are not stuck in toxic environments where luck determines the quality of our relationships.

The second element to familial love relates to those with whom we created a bond with during our childhoods, those with whom we created a sense of community. The catalyst for this element of familial love comes in the form of memories and the fondness we feel when we reflect on those dear and precious times. Our memories preserve these bonds, even if our relationship with the people from our childhood fades over time.

The inclusion of this element to familial love not only teaches us that love expands beyond genetics; it also supports my personal beliefs about family. That our understanding can be redefined within our personal philosophy to acknowledge, embrace, and support ourselves by choosing healthy, loving people to surround ourselves with.

One of the reasons that this element of familial love is so important to me is that it aligns itself with my understanding of Spirit. With a loving Spirit, we discover a fallacy with the idea that family is only genetically based. If family is left to genetics, then it comes down to luck: some people will have wonderful families, and some will be stuck in toxic environments with no way out.

But we know we have a loving creator who supports us. This means that we are not bound by chance or luck determining whether or not we have a happy or fearful life. Familial love can be what we decide. We can share familial love with those who raised us, with those who supported us. We can share familial love with people we have yet to meet designing for ourselves relationships with the potential and probability of health, happiness, and love.

As time passes and we meet our partners and either have or adopt children, we can create a family built on healthy principles. We can create and live our lives based on an expansive and supportive perception (apple) of who family is.

Philia: Friendship Love

The next texture of love we discover in life is philia, or the love of friendship. This love is platonic and comes through the connections we experience with others on a mental level. Rather than butterflies in the stomach or tenderness in the heart for those we have known since birth, friendship love comes through a recognition of connection. You can experience this connection with your neighbors, classmates, cousins, and even a pen pal.

What makes philia a different texture of love, as opposed to storge, is the catalyst that creates this connection. The connection isn't formed through necessity, by being in the same house, or due to being around someone since infancy. Instead, it comes through vulnerability, openness, and action.

Any connection requires a starting point. It can be as simple as a song shared between two people, a favorite TV show, or book series, but this starting off point lends itself to more than a brief connection between two people—it leads to a lasting human connection.

A healthy friendship comes when we are vulnerable, which means we are open to having a connection. Friendship requires us to share something of ourselves. We can recognize an opportunity and a potential for connection, but if we choose not to say hello or develop a relationship through some other form of contact, we will not attain that friendship.

In my research of these ancient Greek terms, I found that part of the definition of "philia" mentions two equal partners. I find this element of philia's definition to be insightful in finding and developing a quality friendship.

A healthy relationship has many different elements, but a healthy friendship adds the element of equality. This definition taught me and put into words what I feel: that friendship is not about a tally sheet or debts but is rather about two people seeing each other as fellow human beings.

Once a connection is felt and embraced, friendship is formed when both people take action. This could mean engaging in deeper conversation, setting plans to meet again, and dedicating time and emotions to bond. With each individual working to develop and maintain a deep connection.

Xenia: Hospitality Love

While we grew up playing hide-and-seek and tag with our friends, our parents were teaching us about basic human kindness, or more widely known as hospitality. This next category of love has two common translations, "guest-friendship" or "ritualized-friendship"; both of these translations help to shed light on xenia.

Within the translation of "xenia" as "guest-friendship," we learn that the term relates to the basic kindness and common courtesies that we display to strangers and acquaintances. We would have first experienced xenia as the corrections and guidance from our parents in our youth: when we encountered adults or strangers and were reminded of the magical importance of "please," and "thank you."

The second most common translation, "ritualized-friendship," sheds light on another element of xenia. Here we see the cultural norms being honored. Our culture doesn't just create structure for us by guiding us towards the correct thing to say and do; at one time, xenia was born of love.

Long ago, we as human beings came together and connected as villages. During this time, we created customs and social norms to not only create harmony but to communicate affection for the community that we were a part of. It was the original form of patriotism.

As time passed these cultural norms shifted and transformed to reflect the evolution of the human race. Men would stand up when a woman entered the room to communicate respect and in more violent nations to communicate protection for a female they knew. People clinked glasses not just in celebration but to slosh the drink around and prove no one was trying to poison anyone else. Holidays were occasions on which to celebrate life and re-birth, and presents were exchanged.

Now, hundreds of years later these social expectations and odd traditions, sayings, and holidays have lost some of their history and importance. Not everyone is taught social courtesies, and just like any texture to love, we must first learn it before we can show it.

So, whether it's xenia or philautia (self-love) we must first learn about these textures of love. It is only then that we can share our hearts with ourselves and with the world around us.

Meraki: Creative Love

While the other ancient Greek categories of love center around our relationships with other people, the modern Greeks have added an additional texture to life. This new addition is derived from the

Turkish "merak." Love, creativity, and devotion are the recipe when we choose to do something with meraki.

In childhood we participated in school art projects with meraki. This enthusiasm teaches us that proficiency and capability are not required in order for us to love what we do. Whether it is an art project or merely making dinner or gardening, whenever we approach an activity in our life with love, creativity, and devotion, we not only create something imbued with love, but we have honored a passion within us and spent our time immersed in meraki.

Ludus: Playful Love

Friendship comes with a connection on a mental level, but ludus, or playful love, comes when we experience butterflies. This texture to love is often what we experience next after friendship.

While it might take a few years, there comes a time in school when our stomach starts to do this funny, twitching kind of thing. Maybe it's because of a girl, maybe it's because of a boy, but in either case, we will soon come to learn that that twitching in our stomach indicates a brand-new experience for us.

Ludus, or playful love, is the affection that we experience with young love. This flirting and teasing euphoria indicates the early stages of romantic love. That being said, the ancient Greeks gave this texture of love its own category because even though we might experience butterflies, it doesn't necessarily mean that we will go on to experience erotic love.

I found this category of love to be the most insightful in my journey of discovering love, because this texture of love comes from our inner child. We experience playful love in the silliness and giddiness that is born from a childlike innocence.

The important component to this love is its catalyst, or foundation. In approaching new love from this childlike space, we discover two important elements to playful love. The first is learning how romantic love will shift and change through different stages.

Romantic love always starts with the potential for a familial love kind of connection. Now, remember that familial love comes through that child-like innocence, that connection we experience before the practical and rational love-or-fear-based philosophy comes into play. Because of the child element to this love, we learn that romantic love has the potential to create a familial bond.

The second element to ludus is the importance it plays in our life. In my research, I discovered that ludus not only appears as butterflies in the stomach, but it is what helps keep life interesting and keeps us engaged throughout our lives. I discovered that no matter how old we become, we need to remain in connection with our inner child in order to experience the youth and vitality that is available to us in a prosperous life.

Eros: Erotic Love

As we continue to grow, there will come a day when the butterflies in our stomach graduate to a deeper, more mature love. This is when we experience eros, or erotic love. Due to the strength and depth of love that we experience within this texture, it has come to play a major role in most people's lives.

The catalyst for this love comes via our physical body and the connection that we experience with certain people. Due to the strength of our physical response, we can also experience loss of control and a desire that can carry us away.

While this Greek category of love focuses solely on the physical sensations we experience from the touch of a lover, I would like to note that there is much more that goes on in a romantic relationship.

Since a romantic relationship has the potential for growth and a long-term experience, it not only encompasses erotic love, but other categories and textures, as well. As we saw with ludus, the beginning of romance starts with butterflies that are born from our inner child. We also develop philia, a strong friendship—not to mention pragma, which we'll take a look at next.

Our romantic relationships encompass many categories and textures. Most people actively seek out these relationships for their potency. Due to the depth and varying styles that this texture of love offers, we can spend years discovering the many layers to eros.

My final note on this category of love is to encourage you to consider what eros means to you. Next, consider what eros means when seen through the eyes of philautia (self-love).

Pragma: Enduring Love

While there are ten Greek categories to love, this is the last healthy category, and pragma is the last texture of love we will discover in life. The catalyst for this love comes from time.

Pragma is the love we discover when we develop a lasting relationship with a loved one. For the couples who make it, this is the love that creates harmony and weaves two people's lives together. The interesting element to this love is that it can only come through intention. Flirtation and even familial love can come naturally and even accidentally.

But pragma is when two people dedicate and work to create a relationship where they actively weave their lives together. This dedication doesn't happen just on their wedding day but happens every day before, during, and after. While I mention married couples, pragma can also be found in deep friendships and strong familial bonds.

The reason this love can be the most elusive is that through time, people change, and so the melding we experience in a relationship can become uneven, split, stretch, or even bow beneath the weight of distance and growth. Which is why a continual refinement and renewal is required. Most of the time, pragma is a healthy style of love simply because of the investment of time it requires, the intention behind the relationship, and the conscious action of maintaining a connection with someone else.

Mania: Obsessive Love

When we chose a seed of love, we took the time to consider what kind of love we wanted for our Heart-Centered Life. We discussed the importance of authenticity so that we could love every aspect of ourselves and others and we also talked about the need for a healthy kind of love. Now, as we've seen with the other nine categories of love, there are many layers and textures to a healthy authentic love.

There is also a texture to love that isn't healthy. So, you might be wondering why I'm talking about it at all. The reason I address this category of love is that knowledge is empowering. Rather than accidentally bumping into an unhealthy love, if we know elements to an unhealthy love, we can see the warning signs, we can understand where it's coming from, and we can make decisions to avoid a potentially painful experience and fear-based lifestyle.

Keeping that in mind let's take a look at the tenth Greek category of love, mania, or manic love. This form of love comes from an imbalance between eros (erotic love) and ludus (playful love), creating a form of madness. Due to this, a person experiencing mania can become possessive, jealous, co-dependent, violent, aggressive, and even dictatorial.

Manic love comes from a place of insecurity, born from the need for self-rescue from low self-esteem. As a result, people who experience manic love place their needs and worth onto other people in order to experience a sense of value.

What makes this love dangerous is that in placing your value on someone else's opinion of you, you place control of your life into someone else's hands. Your worth then becomes dependent on the external world.

As we've discovered, our internal world is the only place we have complete control, and the external world is where we share, influence, and co-create the world we live in. Manic love comes from a place of fear.

Fear pushes people to create these relationships and then pushes them to control the person they are in a relationship with, in order to keep the value that they have obtained. But because control of another person isn't possible, the manic lover lives in this perpetual state of fear.

Since the manic lover's needs are placed onto the shoulders of another person, the manic lover must become more and more possessive in order to survive. To that end, a manic love is not a true relationship between two people. That being the case we need to avoid practicing, and being victims of, manic love.

We cannot find self-worth through another person, but through self-acceptance and self-love. The process of connecting, accepting, and loving yourself happens on a personal level. No matter how much love we give or how much time we put in, only the person experiencing manic love is in the position to make the necessary changes.

When someone enters into a co-dependent relationship with a manic lover, it is essential that they realize that they don't possess the ability to fix the manic lover's problems. In order for this person to practice self-love, they must walk away and get safe. Every human being's safety matters.

It is from these ten categories that we discover love and discover the various shapes and sizes of this vast emotion. While it is a word we can freely use, it is one that we need to sit with and ponder. We must think critically about love and all of its textures if we are to learn how to embrace and utilize it to our benefit.

Based on what you have read in this chapter, how do you understand the two types and ten categories of love? How can you take this understanding and apply it to your relationships, perceptions, and lifestyle moving forward?

Chapter Five Takeaways: Understanding Love

- There are two types (unconditional and conditional love) and ten categories to love. Within these different styles, there are many textures to love.
- Unconditional love is what we share with the world. This quality of love not only transforms the manner in which we live and the world that we help create, but it also keeps us safe.
- Conditional love combines the two truths, that our well-being matters and there are still wounding people out there. This manifestation of self-love helps us navigate to our inner circle.

CHAPTER 5: UNDERSTANDING LOVE

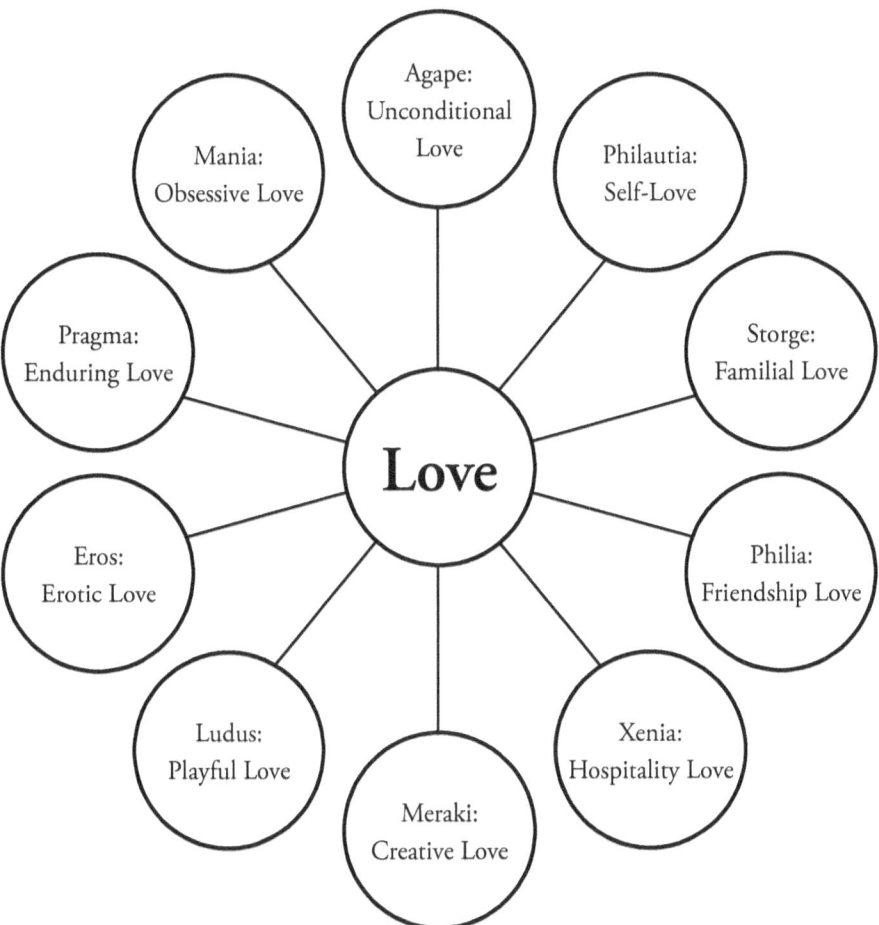

- Due to the transformations that occur when we begin to live life based upon a Heart-Centered lifestyle, we can feel overwhelmed and spent with the idea of loving the world in its entirety. As a result, we utilize our Spoonful Analogy to guide us as we learn to share our love with ourselves, family, and the world around us.
- We can utilize these different categories not only to develop a greater understanding of love, but to integrate this comprehension into our communication, perception, life, and relationships.

CHAPTER 6

A Being of Love, The Nature of Love

my heart shatters
expanding past
the boundaries
of what I know

at first, I cry out
worried that I will fall
that my heart is broken
beyond all repair

but as I breathe
the moment passes
and I find that I am
still alive

for when my heart shatters
I experience a love
past what I knew

I live in a different world where all we are is embraced. Since the start of our healing journey, we have been changing. This change has occurred in tandem with our change in understanding, except we have yet to address the specifics of this transformation. By embracing our authentic love and choosing to heal, we create a Heart-Centered Life.

As a result, we become different people. We become beings of love. As our nature changes, we begin to step into a new world merely as a natural byproduct.

As we...
- Have a healthy understanding of life;
- Love authentically;
- See and understand the world differently,

our weaving with the external world changes.

What we attribute to "human nature" is often times related to the fear seed. When we operate from a seed of love, our responses and interactions with the world transform. We stop playing the fear game and in doing so, we reconnect with our inherit power.

As we consider all we have come to learn about the nature, the styles, and the textures of love, we can see that any life starts with us. Our internal selves will determine what type of life we live.

A happy life.
A life of love.

We start by transforming into beings of love, then we transform how we understand the world on a daily basis. These transformations change what we say and do, and therefore, what type of life we live.

Your life is on your own terms. Its creation and daily perpetuation and maintenance starts with you. You possess the power over your internal reality and thus, the power over your life.

Will you live a thriving human experience?

Fear Seed's Game

In mentioning the transformation we are experiencing, I brought up fear's game. Now, you might be wondering what I'm referring to. In the process of putting together my thoughts about love, I kept running into the knowledge that in living a life of fear, we never stop surviving, even when the situation we are in changes.

This perpetuation of survival, this need to fight and be right, led me to understand the toxic environment that a life based on fear creates. When life is about survival, a division between people occurs. Limited resources and the fear of limited resources both carry the potential to create a world where some people live and some people don't.

On an emotional level, this creates an environment where there are those in power and those who are disempowered. This is what fear's game is—it's about who will come out on top.

Except there's one major problem with this way of life. When you play the game of fear, you lose. It's as simple as that, but yet it holds massive influence over the quality of one's life.

Conclusion
When you play fear's game, you lose.

Argument

In an environment based on fear, there are two main paths a person's life can take. The first is the path of loss. People who end up on the path of loss become disempowered emotionally, mentally, and even physically. They become the victims of bullies, limited resources, and of a lifestyle where they are stuck in survival mode. It's very easy to see how people lose in this fear-based environment.

On the second path, people experience an environment of wealth. Yet in a fear-based society and environment, the feeling and drive for survival persists. It is in this instance where you win fear's game by having the resources, money, food, and power, and yet still lose. Why?

Because now there is a perpetuation of an environment and a lifestyle of fear. People are not able to live a life of prosperity because their need for survival still exists, and because their strength comes from other people's weakness.

As we can see, when we choose to live our lives from a place of fear, we lose. We can lose by losing our power or we can lose by losing our peace of mind and our conscience. Neither environment allows for nor supports prosperity, love, community, global growth, or hope.

While a Heart-Centered Life can be strange to consider and even challenging, at times, to live, it's worth it just so that we have the chance to thrive. To step away from fear and an eternity of survival and fighting, and to step into a life and world that Spirit designed for us.

CHAPTER 6: A BEING OF LOVE, THE NATURE OF LOVE

What It Means to be Good

As things currently stand, the words "good," "bad," "light," and "darkness," inhabit two forms: what they are and how we perceive them, which is to say how we understand them based on what society has taught us.

Ordinarily, society creates for us a playbook to guide us in social interaction, as well as to foster a sense of community among people. But as you saw in the beginning of this book, our current society has rejected a lot of humanity. As a result, many live their lives splintered, lost from themselves and from a happy life. Due to this state of separation, how many people consider themselves good? Are you good?

Since I was a child, I have struggled with identifying my own worth. I've felt at odds with who I am, all of who I am, and what society has taught me about "goodness."

How could I believe in my worth and goodness when hurricanes live inside of me? Tornados and tidal waves have been known to crash within me. When society teaches "good" to be the gentle sweetness, the niceness, the things that are safe, and I have a rolling thunder trembling within me, how can I be good? Parts of me are good, but what about the rest of me?

And here, ladies and gentlemen, is where we have our problem, a misunderstanding of what it means to be good. Right now, we are being taught an idea of good based on a seed of fear. Here, any and all personality traits and emotions that are wild, uncontrollable, and perhaps unsafe or dangerous are rejected, including the primitive parts of ourselves.

These pieces of ourselves are being pushed out of the light and into the darkness. But human beings are both of those things: the gentle soul and the primitive animal.

We can discover a new "good" when we view our lives with love. By taking all that has been rejected and all that has lived in the light, and reuniting these pieces of ourselves, we can achieve a new state of good.

So, what does good mean now?

It means being part of the solution and not the problem. Good isn't synonymous with perfect. Mistakes will be made—that's human error—but goodness is about intentions, words, and actions. Goodness is about choosing growth rather than being afraid to improve or heal.

There are some people out there who are gentle, sweet, and kind. To be harsh, angry, and volatile would be a struggle and a stretch. But they're not the only ones who are good.

For those of us who spark lightning, it's about how we go about honoring ourselves. Too many times we link emotions with words or actions; we see anger as hitting someone or jealousy as insulting comments. But actions or words are merely ways of expressing emotions we feel, thus honoring ourselves. There exists a plethora of other options on how to act or what to say.

Being good means honoring who you are and what you feel (self-love) in a way that matches who you desire to be (quality of character). This way, you aren't hurting others, and you're still part of the solution. By choosing healthy actions and words, you honor the truth of who you are and how you feel without intentionally hurting others in the process. You can be both a good person and a person who still honors the earthquakes inside.

Take a moment to look at yourself in this new light. See the trauma that you have sustained and combine it with the Special Truth that you are unique and important. Then you can begin to see yourself in a whole new light. You can begin to embrace a seed of love and all that is within you.

The Darkness in Our Healing Journey

In the very beginning of this book, I talked about how our life of love means embracing every component of humanity—even the components that society has rejected and pushed into the darkness.

What have you encountered about yourself so far? What kind of scars, wounds, and even mistakes have you encountered in your memories, in your thoughts, and when you look in the mirror?

At this time it's important to note how deeply entrenched fear has become based on what society and our local community has taught us. We can become habitual knee-jerkers, and so a subconscious reaction of rejection, shame, and guilt is not uncommon when you see the entirety of your personality. It is not easy to look deeply at these parts of yourself that you yourself have rejected, believing you needed to reject them in order to be loved by others or even by yourself.

So, I'd like to take this moment to say that no matter what, it is essential that you keep going. This is one of those moments where you are in the darkest parts of the journey. You are so deeply into the tunnel that you cannot see the light ahead, but if you stop here, you'd merely leave yourself in a world of fear and rejection. Push forward and you will come to know and discover a life where the earthquake, the lightning, the calm, and the gentle are all components of your love. Where every aspect of yourself is embraced and honored, cherished and loved.

I've not always enjoyed what I've discovered about myself. Harsh truths, wounded ego, battered pride have all triggered in me a fear response as opposed to a loving one. And I have needed to step back, slow myself down, and re-teach myself how to see things with loving eyes and a loving heart.

Releasing that old seed and embracing a new one can bring us to a crossroads in our own lives. We can continue as we have been, but if we did, we would never achieve the life we dream.

As we've discussed since Volume One, we are striving for a thriving human experience. In order to accomplish this goal, we must make certain changes. When we change the seed that we use, we alter our life.

A thriving human experience requires us to heal in order to dig out the roots that grew from the seed of fear. It requires us to nurture ourselves, too, to help our seed of love blossom, to stretch its roots so that it can reach every aspect of our lives.

The talk is easy, the idea may even be beautiful, but the reality is something altogether new. I have not discussed this yet, but healing has a wide range of experiences.

It's akin to a scratch that bled. It can hurt, and as it heals, it can itch, be painful, annoying, and frustrating. Our wound can be in the most inconvenient spot. The same is true for emotional, mental, and even spiritual healing.

We are addressing wounds, giving voice to things that we may have neglected or buried, and it can be easy to turn up the dial of self-hate, but this is an opportunity to choose a different path. To choose self-love and seek help so you don't walk this path alone. To choose to keep journeying with me so that together, we can achieve all that we have dreamed.

CHAPTER 6: A BEING OF LOVE, THE NATURE OF LOVE

Pulling the Elements of Love Back Together: The Power of Love

Each society tells their populace a story about love. Through movies, literature, and lifestyle, they create and perpetuate a culture of love. If you were to look at my society, you would find love depicted as loyalty to family, no matter the quality of their character. You would find grand gestures to convey love and either a highly rational approach to romantic love (check-lists and resumés) or non-rational responses that are justified by platitudes like, "I have no choice" or "I had to." Yet is this the truth?

I recently came across an essay by Russian sociologist Polina Aronson titled "Romantic Regimes." In her essay, she introduced the idea of Romantic Regimes as "Systems of emotional conduct that affect how we speak about, how we feel, determine 'normal' behaviors, and establish who is eligible for love—and who is not."

Essentially, we are each raised within a type of romantic regime determined by our society and culture. The external world has a powerful influence over all of us. Due to this influence, our cultures create a story about love. It teaches us the whys and how comes. It influences how we understand, perceive, and approach love in our daily lives. It was from Polina Aronson's essay that I learned just how differently various cultures perceive this one texture of love.

What this taught me was that in a society based on fear, love gets splintered and separated in order to obscure the strength that can be found within it. What's puzzling is that society does this with fear, as well, not to reduce the strength of fear, but to disguise it so that we place more fear into our lives than we might be aware of at first.

Fear not only has the power to overwhelm us, but acts as an unhealthy seed, spreading into every area of our lives. Love has this same capacity to spread into every area of our lives, but it does so in a healthy way, where we experience support no matter where we are or what we're doing. As we develop a Heart-Centered Life, we will take the time to delve deep into the layers and textures of love. We will re-identify lost components of love, just as we have with fear.

We saw that fear can be misidentified as practicality or safety. Fear is a massive and versatile emotion. Unless we take the time to analyze and get to know the various elements of fear, we run the risk of misidentifying them and letting elements of fear remain in our lives unnecessarily.

The same is true for love. By taking the time to analyze and get to know the many qualities of love, we will uncover…

- New experiences.
- Greater love and happiness.
- The strength of love.

For Example: Tenderness

Love is more than enjoyment of chocolate or connection to family. When we discussed manic love, we uncovered the combination of fear plus love. While this is an unhealthy love, it shows us how love can be combined and shaped to create a full life.

With love, we have courage. Love and courage together create compassion. With love and hope, we have a stronger faith, a dedication to elements unseen and unproven. With love, we have grand gestures and intense emotions, but there is also the capacity for tenderness.

Tenderness comes when we combine gentleness with love. When we practice tenderness, we uncover a sweetness in life. Now,

CHAPTER 6: A BEING OF LOVE, THE NATURE OF LOVE

tenderness on its own is not a foreign term or experience. But did you know it's a form of love?

In a society of fear, love has been splintered into different categories and elements in order to disguise the strength that it has. In delving into love for our Heart-Centered Life, we can pull all of these different facets of love back together to not only enrich our lives, but to help us uncover the power of love.

This power strengthens our lives and provides us with the ability to say no to fear, to stop playing the game of fear, and to step away from a fear-based lifestyle.

As a direct result we become empowered, and we place ourselves in a position where we can not only experience a prosperous human life, but we can also greatly confuse those who would wish us harm, removing their power to push our buttons. In doing so, they lose the power to dictate a life of fear for us and for our community.

We see evidence of this reconnected love, the strength of it and the power of it, in one of my heroes, Mahatma Gandhi. As a student and teacher of nonviolence, he led not only his own people but others to freedom. Can you imagine the strength necessary to stand and take a beating and not harm the other person?

From a perspective of fear, this is an insane and illogical action, but when we look through the eyes and heart of love, we uncover the strength that freedom fighters and non-violent protestors used. The wrongs and disempowerment that people experienced was unjust. Yet these people chose a course of action that demonstrated the quality of their character and the strength that they had to say "no" to the fear people were trying to push into their hearts.

There are still wounded people in this world, and we still witness and uncover instances of unjust action. These instances can trigger anger and hatred in our hearts. It is in these moments when a life of compassion and love can seem the most illogical and unwise of choices.

Through our healing journey we are transforming into beings of love. We are ending the perpetual cycle of injustice. We are also uncovering a strength to acknowledge injustices that break our heart. We are discovering a strength and immovable integrity within us to do something about these injustices, to take action, not to rail against the unmovable and unchangeable past, but to invest our energy into a present and a future where we are an equal community.

Forgiveness

When I began to make changes to my life, I took the time to consider what sort of life I wanted to live. As a result, I discovered that I wanted my life to be filled with love, happiness, freedom, and safety. I didn't want to be prisoner to a life of pain. I wanted to be free to be at peace. As I move forward with my life, more of my time is spent being happy and grateful.

This insight into what I wanted my life to look and feel like guided me as I made changes. As a direct result, my life has become healthier and less toxic. I emulate more of my inner child's wonder and glee. But in order to achieve this state, I've needed to stop carrying around emotions and thoughts that no longer serve me well.

I have needed to forgive and move on, releasing my victim mentality, releasing my need for revenge, and releasing my hatred, fear, and anger. This has been a challenge.

For a long time, I thought that forgiveness was just hard, until I followed my understanding of forgiveness back to its source. Its seed.

CHAPTER 6: A BEING OF LOVE, THE NATURE OF LOVE

As you may have guessed, I found that my understanding of forgiveness was all tangled up in and distorted by fear. At that time, I saw forgiveness as letting the other person off the hook. I was communicating to those who had wounded me that I was ok with their actions. But that's not what it's about at all.

Due to my misunderstanding, I wasn't forgiving people or myself. I discovered that forgiveness requires us to address what happened and accept it. Many times, forgiveness was *not* a path I chose because I did not want to address the truth of a painful moment. I still wanted the chance to re-write life and avoid pain.

I realized that living a happy life simply means that I spend more time being happy. I also realized that in order to experience happiness, I needed to release certain outdated and now irrelevant emotions. By breaking down my desires into the steps and changes needed, I uncovered not only a misunderstanding in my idea of forgiveness, but a place where I had splintered from myself.

The Danger of Not Forgiving

By splitting ourselves into the past and future, we sever the connection we have with the present, where life is actually happening. When we're angry or unwilling to forgive, so many things happen at the same time, and all of these things wound us in different ways.

Firstly, we trap ourselves in a victim mentality. We push away power that we could be utilizing to make changes, to stop the pain, and live a prosperous life.

Secondly, we pull ourselves apart by carrying the past into the present. When we do this, we are painting the present, thus placing a block between what we desire from the present and what we get. As we paint the present with the emotions of the past, we take this untouched, limitless possibility that we have in the present and influence it in a negative manner.

By choosing not to forgive, be it others or ourselves, we are choosing a course of action that works against the life we envision for ourselves. We place a block between ourselves and the life we desire.

What is Forgiveness?

In order to successfully forgive, we need to understand what forgiveness means as well as the process we'll utilize to do so.

The first step is to honor the truth of the moment. When we honor our emotions, we honor ourselves and practice self-love.

What wound was inflicted? What words were said? What actions were taken that violated your free will, your freedom, your heart, your mind, your body?

Next, how are you honoring your emotions? Did you speak up for yourself and say what needed to be said? Did you take action and walk away? If you were unable to walk away, did you protect yourself or express displeasure? Can you safely do something now if you were unable to do something then? Can you honor your emotions in a way that reflects the type of person you want to be?

Once you honor the emotion in a way that aligns with who you choose to be or what you are capable of in that moment, it is time to release the emotion so that you are ready and open to the next emotion that will come with the next moment. This transition into a new moment brings you to a place where you are not a victim but have the potential to experience healing and happiness.

To forgive means to release the burden of that moment and set it down into the past, where it will not taint future moments, hold

CHAPTER 6: A BEING OF LOVE, THE NATURE OF LOVE

you down moving forward, or be a weight upon your shoulders. It is not a way of saying it was ok, because it wasn't ok.

In saying, "I accept your apology," or by looking inward, we can relinquish the moment so that it may end and a new moment can enter our lives—quite possibly a happier and healthier moment. This is how we forgive.

Self-Forgiveness

The forgiveness of others revolves around acceptance and releasing the feeling of powerlessness for a better moment. But forgiving ourselves is a little different.

I have found that when it comes to my own self, I am less capable of forgiveness than I am with others. My emotions cloud my mind and sometimes I don't understand myself. Yet, I can interact with others and see clearly what their heart is feeling.

Due to the murky world of self-analysis, self-forgiveness can be challenging for the simple reason that we don't see our own human-ness, our own ability to make mistakes. We can also choose to beat ourselves up when we encounter a moment of weakness.

Sometimes, we make a choice that we know isn't in our best interest or isn't kind to ourselves or others. Other times, we look back at our lives and hold our past selves to the same standards that we utilize today. This is why self-forgiveness requires a slightly different process. Just like forgiving others, forgiving ourselves takes a willingness. Are you willing to let go of old emotions, see the complexity of human life, and return to the present moment where life is happening?

The first step in self-forgiveness is to acknowledge the truth of what happened. Whether recent or in the past, what happened? What mistake did we make?

Next, we must *accept* the truth. The past can't be re-written, and it is more healing when we accept the past. If we choose to invest our energy into combating the truth of the past, we will still be unable to change anything, and we end up exhausted and no better off.

Once we accept what has happened and what we have done, we need to look at the surrounding actions, words, thoughts, and philosophy at play. Why did we act that way? In self-analyzing, we might come across a rotten apple, a wound we didn't know we had, or even a hidden emotion we were unaware of.

While it can be challenging to delve into the moment of self-inflicted pain or pain we've inflicted on others, doing so will shed light onto the nature of events. It is in these moments that we are presented an opportunity to discover more about ourselves, heal, remove a rotten apple, and to grow—and we must seize them.

It is important to make mention at this time that we not hold our past selves to the same standards that we hold our current selves. Right now, you are operating with new knowledge and a new personal philosophy, things you didn't have in the past. When looking back, consider what you knew then, and how that understanding of life and yourself influenced how you acted and what you said.

Lastly, forgive. Take this opportunity to live a Heart-Centered Life and demonstrate self-love and kindness towards yourself. As human beings, we have a right to be imperfect.

CHAPTER 6: A BEING OF LOVE, THE NATURE OF LOVE

A World of Emotions

In Volume One, we entered a world of philosophy. We considered topics and ideas and put them to the test. Through rational thought and a couple leaps of faith, we put together a bedrock for our personal philosophy. Now we have entered into a world of emotions. The reason we are focusing on emotions is twofold.

Firstly, emotions are how we, as human beings, experience life. Our five senses, the sensations of touch, sound, sight, smell, and taste, vary based on how we respond to external stimuli. The texture and flavor we experience when eating chocolate, the feeling of bare feet on the grass, or the sound of violins elicit a different response from each of us. As you can see, our experience of life comes down to the emotional response we have to the situation or the moment we are living in.

The reason we are basing our Heart-Centered Life around our emotions is because we learn, change, and grow. So, the quality of our life is determined by our experiences but is maintained by the emotions we feel in relation to those experiences.

Let me explain myself. As a child, comfort food like Mac-and-Cheese triggered feelings of tenderness and hominess. As we grow and our palette changes, different foods will bring about that emotion of tenderness and hominess. While the foods of our childhood hold a special place in our hearts, they may not elicit the same response as time passes.

Therefore, to live a thriving human experience, our focus is actually on the emotions we experience. As we've seen from the experiences of our childhood, the situations and moments that elicit the emotions we want (love, happiness, safety, etc.) change as we change.

So, rather than returning to what worked for us before or even returning to the past or an old relationship, we must seek out the emotion we desire instead. We are basing our personal philosophy on emotions because they will act as a consistent framework for us moving forward.

If we created the framework with situations or experiences, as time passed, those situations and experiences may no longer be accurate in eliciting the same emotional response. Engaging in the same stimuli that we sought in the past might not mean we're living a happy life today.

With that in mind, we will structure the definitions of what we seek in life around the emotions we desire. While the food or the activity might change, our structure and the work we're putting in will remain relevant to us not only today but in the days to come, as we transform even more.

Put it to the Test

Consider for a moment how you feel about emotions and their importance. As we continue on our healing journey, I encourage you to always put what you read to the test, not only to make sure you're gathering wisdom, but also because what you need from life and what I need from life are two separate things, as we are two separate individuals.

Do you understand why we want to base our personal philosophy on emotions rather than places, people, things, and foods? Do you agree with this conclusion, or does it need to be altered to work for you?

CHAPTER 6: A BEING OF LOVE, THE NATURE OF LOVE

The Internal and External World's Impact on Love

Not only are there many layers to our emotions, but each experience itself holds different elements that impact our lives in different ways. As we've seen with love, there are many textures and layers to this one emotion. But there's also more going on in a single moment than what meets the eye.

Within a single moment, we not only experience a single emotion like love, but many other emotions, as well. This specialized concoction of emotions creates a unique experience for us in life. Not only does this mean that each moment of our lives has the potential to be unique and engaging, but it also brings about layers to the moment we are experiencing.

The layering of emotions and the impact of our internal and external realities creates the complexities found within life. Which is why I am going to share a personal moment from my life, breaking down not only the specialized concoction of emotions I experienced, but also the impact my internal and external realities had on the truth of those emotions.

In college, I took a public speaking class. Truthfully, I took the class because it was taught by my interpersonal communications teacher. He was a wonderful and informative teacher, and I thought it might provide for an interesting experience. I didn't know at the time how vital the information I learned would be to my new career. (There's that soul contract coming into play.)

As the name of the class suggests, we spent a quarter learning about the elements of speech and practicing in front of the class. The first speech we gave needed to be eight to ten minutes long, about a subject of our choosing.

The day of the speech I arrived at class with a stack of notecards in hand and dressed in a professional looking outfit. When it was my turn to speak, I gathered my notes, stood up, and walked to the front of the class.

In this moment of my life, I experienced a unique concoction of emotions...
- Excitement
- Nervousness
- Shyness
- Curiosity
- Anxiety
- Worry
- Hope
- Along with some more minor emotions.

Not only was I excited to talk about animal totems (a form of spirit guides), but I was also nervous to be speaking in front of my class about a topic that would probably get mixed responses. In that moment, I was also anxious to know what my teacher would think and hopeful that at the end of my speech, my grade would be satisfactory.

As I stood in front of my class and gave my speech, all of these emotions raged inside of me. At the same time, my breathing was fast, I had some sweat under my armpits, I tried to keep my hands from shaking, I kept shifting my weight back and forth between my legs, and time seemed to move at a glacial speed.

All of these things happened in this ten-minute period of time, and all of the emotions I felt were real. Not only did this concoction of emotions create a unique moment in my life, but there were two truths happening at once.

This is where we see the impact of our internal and external worlds. As we discussed in Volume One, our internal world is all that exists within us. This is our emotions, thoughts, feelings, ideas, perceptions, and our personal philosophy. On the other hand, our external reality is the world we co-create.

One truth is all that I experienced within my internal world. All the emotions, the thoughts, the worries and concerns, and the realization I would need to do this more than once.

The second truth is all that occurred in the external world. While all the emotions I felt within me were real, the external world held a slightly different truth: the truth that I was composed, professional, fluent, and poised.

Can you see how these two truths, combined with the concoction of emotions I felt, not to mention the emotions others were feeling, create a complexity to life?

In a single moment of our life, all of these different elements exist. We have emotions, thoughts, ideas, and perceptions, all within ourselves, combined with everything everybody else is feeling and thinking, and then what we and others communicate through actions and words in the external world.

Expressing Emotions

During my first speech, there were the emotions I felt and the emotions that the external world witnessed. In the process, we get to see the two truths to what we feel. Both are important, yet the impact of our emotions on the external world is determined by one thing: communication.

While all of my anxiety and worry was real for me, no one in my class would have known what I was feeling unless I communicated it. There are many ways we communicate our emotions, but as we saw with my story, in order for your emotions to be real in the external world, they must be communicated.

If we want to live a thriving human experience, we need to communicate how we feel. That's one way we weave our lives into the world around us and create authentic human connection.

We can communicate our emotions in a number of ways: through words, tone, sentence structure, and volume, we express how we feel. We can also express emotions through actions and gestures. This is how our emotions become real in the external world.

Expressing our emotions is the only way others will know how we feel. Since we are not mind readers, communicating emotions helps people make informed choices in interactions, relationships, and even negotiations.

Communicating how we feel is the first step in connecting more deeply with our community. In the past, you might not have considered all the emotions that you felt in each moment. In a life based on fear, the drive for survival limits what we can experience and how much of ourselves we can honor.

We are often preoccupied with the need to keep ourselves alive, to survive moment to moment, and as such don't take the time to get in touch with how we feel (that authentic love for every aspect of ourselves). Nor do we feel safe to convey the multi layering of emotions we feel. On account of this, we often answer with one emotion (happy, good, bad) when asked how we feel.

But we are no longer living a life of fear. Instead, we have stepped into a world of love. As we transform and become beings of love, we create a new environment for ourselves where we start embracing all the emotions that we experience and start living in an environment where we feel safe to express and honor these emotions.

Communicating Our Emotions

After we identify how we feel, the next step is to consider how we will communicate our emotions. It is important to consider how we communicate and honor our emotions for two reasons.

When we experience an emotion, we also make a choice. We choose an action or a series of words to accurately convey how we feel. But with each emotion there comes a myriad of choices. The actions we choose to take or words we choose to speak convey not only how we feel, but the quality of our character, as well—whether we are a kind or an angry type of person.

The second reason we must consider how we communicate our emotions is that not every action or word choice means the same thing to everyone. Conveying our emotions makes them real in the external world we all share; conveying them in a way that is clear and direct helps people to understand how we feel. Without this clarity in communication, there is a potential for great confusion.

Ways We Express Love

We each have a personal preference in how we communicate love. In upholding our own personal preference, we not only honor ourselves, but we also honor our special expression of love, unique to who we are.

So, while we express love in a myriad of ways given the object of our affection, situation, or context, we each have personal preferences. By knowing the different ways we express love, and the perceived pros and cons, you can communicate more effectively with those you cherish.

Words

Many people mark the cementing of their relationship with the phrase, "I love you." With various words and phrases, we communicate the depth, quality, strength, and reasons why we love one another.

Pro

Some people choose to express their love through words due to the large vocabulary available to them and the desire to be clear and specific. This declaration not only shares love with a loved one, but also makes this love public knowledge.

Con

Although vocalization is a common style and tool for expressing love, it doesn't work for everyone. As I mentioned above, just because an action or phrase conveys how we feel, it doesn't necessarily mean that the other person will translate our actions or words in the same way.

For some people, expressing their love through words can be challenging. This might be due to shyness or because they view words as ephemeral. Words can be lies. So, when expressing something as deep and profound as love, words fail.

The choice to avoid words might be caused by a moment of heartbreak in the past, or a personal experience that led a person to see words as unreliable. Someone else's experiences with verbal communication might have had the opposite effect on their personal opinions.

Touch

The second most notable expression of love is physical touch. Hugs, kisses, cuddling, handholding, and even massages can be used to express love. Physical action and touch are integral parts of expressing love for many of us, especially since we are pack animals.

Pro

Allowing another person into your personal space to hold and support you indicates vulnerability and trust. But just as this style is my favorite, it can be another's least.

Con

Others can have larger physical, personal boundaries, where hugs and kisses become invasive, demanding, and inappropriate annoyances. That's why I not only communicate my affection through touch but look to utilize other ways to express my love.

I not only get to share my love but also respect other's preferences. In doing so, I combine self-love (communicating my emotions) with who I want to be (a kind and respectful person). It also makes the hugs I get from my friends all the more precious.

The Impact of Preference

When I was a child, I didn't know about different ways of expressing love. I was a leaner, needing my mom to let me know when she needed to move so I didn't fall over. I also communicated heartfelt apologizes through hugs. As a young child, getting out the words "I'm sorry" wasn't physically possible—my throat would close up and not let the words pass—but providing a squeezing hug *was* possible.

How we express our emotions comes first through intuition. Some children naturally reach out and others choose to make gurgling noises. We then observe how our family members communicate their emotions and emulate them, not only to fit in but because doing so is all we know. We see and then do, believing that this is how human nature works.

As you continue your healing journey, think back to your first instinct in childhood, as well as how your family responded. Do you share their preference? How can you honor theirs and yours?

Gifts

Following a first kiss, we often choose to give and receive gifts. Flowers, chocolate, jewelry and signed memorabilia all have become common gifts to give loved ones. In the days of old, gifts could take the form of animal skins or animals themselves (like horses). Through time our ideas of gift-giving and romance have changed. Nowadays, we don't need to feel limited by what society currently defines as romantic.

Pro

For some people, the greatest sign you can give to a loved one is to buy and bring home a present. There are few reasons why.
- First: The money. This loved one has worked hard for his/her money and then, despite the limited supply, has chosen to use it to buy something for you.
- Second: The actual gift itself. The gift must then by pondered. While your loved one is picking out a gift for you, they are thinking about you and what you might like.
- Lastly: Buying it. Your loved one must now make a plan, go out of his/her way to purchase the gift, and then hope you'll love it. In doing so, they put their heart on the line.

Con

While the act and presentation of gift giving holds the potential to convey deep emotion, on the other hand, a different person may feel as if you're equating your love for them as equal to that of money. That you are buying off their love without investing any of your own.

As you can see, we have the most success conveying our love in a relationship when both parties are aware of one another's preferences. Not only will there be greater understanding when we get presented with a gift, but we can also combine our dominant method with our loved one's method.

Time

Time is a precious commodity. We cannot buy, steal, or barter an extra hour to add to our day. Even if you are in excellent health, we are all going to die someday. For some people, the greatest way they can show they love you is to spend time with you.

Pro

Someone spending time with you might mean driving over to your place with their paperwork in hand so the two of you can work side-by-side. Making a point to be with you, even with a busy schedule, might be the greatest act of love they know.

Con

Some people need time alone to accomplish their to-do list or to just rest and contemplate life. As such, they prefer to spend time with their loved ones when they are doing or working on the same thing. They don't feel the need to be close even when they are occupied with work.

But if we can look at the actions of a person who communicates their love through time, through their eyes, we can gain clarity in what they are attempting to communicate. They're telling us, "You're so important to me, I want to be near you no matter what it is I am doing."

Support and Aid

For some, the greatest act of love comes in giving assistance—more specifically, helping out with things that are difficult or that we don't like to do. With verbal assistance and tangible action, people help lighten the load of those they love.

Pro

For example, if you hate doing the dishes, your loved one might choose to do them for you. This person will take on the tasks that are hard or distasteful for you, carrying this burden so that your life may be filled with as much happiness as possible.

Con

However, if you are not this person, you might experience frustration. While your loved one is off washing the dishes, you might wish that he/she is sitting next to you as you watch the movie.

Prayer

In Volume One, we discovered that Spirit is a loving and kind creator. From this simple conclusion, we can extrapolate so much knowledge about the nature of life and the tools, guidance, and gifts at our disposal. One such tool is prayer.

By reaching out and communicating to Spirit, we are able to manifest a better world for ourselves and others. We...
- Develop a relationship with a loved one. Each prayer is communication and connection with Spirit.
- Are able to ask for assistance, which reduces, if not eliminates the burden on our shoulders.
- Can ensure that our loved ones are receiving care and aid. Even when we aren't in a position to give them what they need.

Pro

For those of us who have a strong connection to their faith and Spirit, prayer not only helps us send aid to those we love, but also comforts us.

Con

While prayer brings me a sense of peace, for others prayer can be seen as presumptuous, especially when differing beliefs are involved. People can feel forced into a situation, experience, or end result they don't want nor feel comfortable with.

"The Most Benevolent Outcome For All Involved"

I don't know everything, and I don't believe any human being knows everything. Due to this fact, the way we tailor our prayers matters. Long ago, my family healer taught my mother and me the phrase, "Most benevolent outcome."

Essentially, when we pray, we send our desires and wishes out into the Universe with the hope and faith that they'll be answered. Sometimes the facilitator of our prayers is Spirit, our spirit guides, or in other cases, Mother Earth or the Universe.

This form of communication comes from what we, as human beings, know and desire. But as I said, we don't know everything. So, sometimes our prayers won't be answered, not because we are being neglected but because they aren't actually what's best for us or others.

In order to provide aid (the whole point of prayer for others and even for ourselves) the way in which we phrase our prayer matters. Through the use of the phrase "most benevolent outcome," we are able to honor the fact that we don't know.

By asking Spirit for, "the most benevolent outcome for all involved," we are not only asking for the best outcome for others, but for all involved in the situation. We not only succeed in expressing our love, but also do our part in ensuring that what is needed will be provided.

Another reason this wording is extremely helpful is due to the role our soul contracts plays in our lives. Since soul contracts are the plans we made before birth to facilitate opportunities for learning, teaching, and growth, they will influence our life experiences.

Due to the specifics of any person's soul contract, what one needs in a situation might not make the most practical sense. By praying for the most benevolent outcome, we ask for aid for ourselves and our loved ones, while honoring that we don't know the specifics of their lives, their soul contract, or the big picture plan for the world as a whole.

Energy Transfer

The final manner through which we can express our love is via conscious energy work. We discovered the importance of energy in Volume One, and also discovered how we can become conscious energy workers.

By working with energy consciously, we not only determine the quality of our energy work (since we are influencing energy every day), but we can empower ourselves with the opportunity to utilize important tools, like our Six Safety Tools.

Pro

There are times in our lives when we didn't get enough sleep or maybe have a huge project that's due. To support those we love, we sometimes need to give them space to get their work done, but that doesn't mean we can't express our love.

By consciously channeling energy to those we love, we give them a little surge that can help push them or provide them strength when they need it most. What greater act of love is there than sharing the very energy we carry within us?

Con

Just as some people might be inclined to share their energy, others don't want to, or might not even be able to handle such an experience. Between the energy vampires out there, and the different ways in which people process the experience, energy transfers can sometimes be seen and felt as invasive and overwhelming.

If you've ever been in front of a bunch of people (for a speech, recital, concert, etc.), you might have already experienced this kind of energy exchange. While the audience roots for you, they can transfer energy to you subconsciously. Hence why some performers experience a buzz when performing live.

Therefore, I recommend that you talk with your loved ones before sharing energy. For many people, this love expression is new and foreign. It opens up an entirely new layer to human life that not everyone is interested in discovering.

How to Share Energy

Becoming a conscious energy worker ranges from simple, healthy intentions to further development and becoming an energy healer. While energy impacts our lives, you are not required to delve into this new layer unless it is what you wish. You don't need to consciously share energy with others in order to love them. As we've seen, there are so many ways to express your love. As you create a unique style all your own, do so from the perspective of honoring yourself.

Being a conscious energy worker means taking the time to consider the ethical considerations surrounding how we approach and utilize our energy. While energy has always been a part of human life and is an ancient tool of Shamans and Medicine People, it's not something we have talked about.

Due to the rejection and ostracism that this layer to life has received and endured, open discussion of these tools, practices, cultures, and lifestyles has not been safe. That being the case, the discourse surrounding the proper protocol for energy work hasn't happened. Yet…

So, on that note, let me walk you through a visualization exercise that you can use to share your energy with loved ones. Then, I'll break down the whys and how comes so that you can see how this practice is respectful to all.

Energy Sharing Visualization Technique

I always recommend starting any conscious energy work by grounding and shielding. While I utilize these safety tools every day, I like to recheck and sometimes add layers to my shield so that I stay in a healthy and safe place as I do energy work or healing.

Next, visualize a small ball of energy like that of a small sun. You can even take your hands and hold them in front of you, cradling your ball of energy.

Then, visualize who you wish to share this energy with. Stating their name or even thinking their name (first and last) will ensure the energy gets to them. If you just think, "my friend in need," the energy might be sent to a friend who needs it more than the one you had in mind.

Lastly, release this energy from your possession and send it on its way. This step can be accomplished by lightly tossing the energy from your hands, blowing your friend a kiss, giving them a hug, or even just letting go.

The Whys and How Comes

By first grounding and shielding, you are practicing self-love. You are then respectful to your friend based on your intentions. Through the intention of "sharing," you are respecting the wishes of others. You're not placing someone in a position where they "have to" accept the energy, but are rather offering it to them, just as if you were offering assistance.

Through the visualization of a small ball of energy, you are keeping yourself healthy by not giving all the energy you have. You are also not overwhelming the other person with a big ball of sun.

Lastly, treat each time you share energy as an individual occurrence. Just because you've shared energy in the past doesn't mean that this time is the same. And just because someone shared energy with you in the past, doesn't mean they are available or interested this time. When it comes to energy work with other people, communication is key.

Becoming a conscious energy worker changes how you perceive and understand the world. While the tools and techniques are often ancient (although new tools are being discovered and created today), the discussion of the "right way" is being had now.

If you ever encounter a new tool while utilizing energy, are acting as that conscious energy worker, or if you are connecting with a psychic ability, take a moment to consider what you would be comfortable with. Not only today, but when you first discovered energy. While this introspection won't always provide you with the answer as to what is "right," it will help to guide you so that your energy work will be kind and healing, and not harmful.

Balancing Methods of Expression

Who we are is composed of a myriad of traits and preferences that makes each of us unique and special unto ourselves. As a result, we each have a dominant method for expressing our love.

However, this doesn't mean that when we look for a relationship, we must limit it to people who share the same dominant method for expressing love. All that is required is that you know your loved one's dominant style and make a point to at least balance the method you use to express your love. In doing so, you not only make your love real in the external world, but you also help yourself to be better understood by those you love.

Which style of expressing love is your dominant method? Which is the dominant method of your loved ones? How might you balance these methods to better express your love?

CHAPTER 6: A BEING OF LOVE, THE NATURE OF LOVE

When we express our emotions, we make them real in the external world. Whether it is love, pride, appreciation, or any other emotion, our expression helps those around us understand how we feel.

Thinking about the method for expressing your emotions is important, but I want to take a moment to remind you that you are not responsible for another person's life. While you can work to add clarity to your communication, any relationship or interaction requires two participating individuals.

It still requires the other person to be responsible for considering what you are communicating. Just as they represent the external world when they interact with you, you become the external world when interacting with others.

When someone says or does something, oftentimes it is clear what sort of emotion they are expressing. But on those occasions when you are confused or maybe even offended, ask yourself, what emotion might they be trying to communicate? You can even ask them directly and avoid a painful moment.

By taking the time to consider our choices as well as analyze the choices and actions of others, we strengthen the quality of our relationships. As a result, we have a better chance at not only transforming into a loving being, but creating a loving and safe environment for ourselves and others, where we step into this new world and live a Heart-Centered Life.

Chapter Six Takeaways: A Being of Love, The Nature of Love

- Through the healing journey that we are on, we are entering into a new world. We enter into this new world by becoming beings of love.
- By living our lives from this place of love, we stop playing fear's game.
- As we begin to embrace ourselves (light and darkness), our understanding of "good" and "bad" will shift to reflect our new and healthy perception.
- We will also start honoring all the emotions we feel.
- To make the emotions we feel real to the external world, we must express them.
- By choosing the manner in which we express our emotions, we not only honor ourselves but express the quality of our character.

CHAPTER 7

Self-Love

when you fall asleep
you give up the day
to become your shadow self

a stark truth of pain and love
of light and dark
powerful and strong

made by the truth
of who you are
embracing all that is
and all that you can be

it is then upon waking
that we lose sight
and once again
navigate life blindly

yet through time
we can set the intention
to be all we are

no longer a shadow
but colorful and bright

With each step in our healing journey, we delve deeper and deeper into a richer world. On account of this, we not only have built a foundation for our lives, that personal philosophy, but we have begun to acquire knowledge that we can utilize to build a thriving life. As we learned in Volume One and in this volume, knowledge can become a means of stimulating new ideas and achieving new understandings.

When we delved into the styles and textures of love, we began to suss out the many layers of that simple word, one of those layers being self-love. We touched briefly upon how self-love becomes present when we encounter conditional love, and again within the ancient Greek category of philautia. Now it's time to delve deeper into self-love.

As we discovered in Volume One, we exist in two realities: our internal reality and our external reality. When we dove into what that meant, we discovered that our internal reality was within our complete control, and that our external reality was something that we influence and share collective responsibility for.

In having complete control and responsibility of our internal reality, we possess a power to determine the quality of this reality. We can decide if we will be living in pain or living in love. For that reason, self-love becomes a vital component of not only a Heart-Centered Life, but in our healing journey.

There are many books out there with varied understandings of self-love, and here, I will share with you what I have come to learn. As always, put what I share to the test and then take what works for you.

What is Self-Love?

I understand self-love to be the relationship that we have with ourselves. Like any relationship, we step past basic need and enter a world of choice. We are not required to be in a relationship with anybody, so when we choose to enter into a relationship, it is just that: a choice. In making this choice to love ourselves, we see that we have value no matter what the external reality may suggest.

By loving ourselves, we take the time to connect with ourselves. Connecting with ourselves not only means taking care of our body, mind, heart, and soul, but also taking the time to get to know our own personalities. What is it that brings you joy? What brings you pain?

We are then in a position to make decisions that reflect this knowledge. When we do, we can choose the things that we love and find joy in, rather than the things that break our heart. We choose to place a hand over our heart rather than poking ourselves in the eye.

This relationship becomes a lifestyle of self-advocacy. Not only are you navigating your life in a healing way, but you are also taking part in the most powerful relationship you will ever have—for when we consider the nature of the human experience, we'll discover that the only relationship you will have for life, besides the one with Spirit, is the one that you have with yourself.

Take a moment to consider what that means.

When we realize that our relationship with ourselves will last longer than any other relationship, we understand how vital and important this relationship is in our lives. It becomes an integral component to the reality and quality of our thriving existence.

Why Self-Love?

If you're still unconvinced as to the importance of self-love, take a moment to consider not what self-love does for you, but what it does for the world. When we love ourselves, we change the quality and condition of our lives.

In Volume One, we saw how we are all a part of this world. As such, the quality of our lives weaves into this world and not only increases the quality of the world as a whole, but also the quality of those around us. This impact is the influence that each of us as individuals have over our external reality—the world we co-create.

Self-love acts as proof of the community and ecosystem that we share.

First

We heal ourselves through our healing journey and by learning to not only love ourselves but to put our self-love into action. By learning who we are and learning how to self-advocate, we change the manner in which we live our lives. As a result, we improve the quality of our lives.

Secondly

By choosing to facilitate all of these improvements and also learning the various wisdom and tools we need to make these changes, we now possess skills we didn't have before. Not only will these skills aid us in our healing journey, but they also will become skills we can share with the world.

When this happens, we become living, breathing, walking, and talking examples of a better life and a better world. We can also become teachers for those around us.

Changing the World

As a medicine woman, I not only impart change by practicing a healthy Heart-Centered Life, but I also help the world by sharing the wisdom I possess. Like me, we each can impart change by living a life of love as well as choosing healthy activities and tools to live our lives and help the world. This is why I will be sharing various ways through which we can take on a more active role in life. This will help us to impart change and smooth the transition from a fear-based existence into one built upon healthy, authentic love.

One simple way I impart healing and change around me is by taking the time to consider how I weave within the external world. As you know, we are two selves: the internal and the external. The internal is all of who we are (the iceberg); it is through self-love that we honor our complex selves, both the hidden and known aspects. Our external selves are the visible aspects of the iceberg.

As we learn to love ourselves, we can take an additional step to impart change and healing as well. This step is to consider our character, who we are as people, and how we go about weaving with the world—if we will choose to be a part of the solution or part of the problem.

More simply put, this step represents the actions we choose to take and the words we choose to use. Do we utilize our words and actions for harm or for love?

Healing = Changing
- It starts with you because you have complete control and power over yourself.
- You are part of the whole, so your personal human condition matters to you and to the whole.

- You avoid the double standard and hypocrisy of asking others to heal and refusing to do so yourself.
- People learn through stories and examples. By healing yourself, you are utilizing the power of influence that you have on the external world and putting it to positive use.

What Comes From Self-Love?

Let's take a moment to look at the benefits that we enjoy by loving ourselves. For loving ourselves is an investment and a dedication of time and energy, like any relationship.

Love creates a building block for compassion and courage. It becomes that driving force, so that when we are faced with a decision, we will be in a place where we have the power and the commitment to choose the things that will bring us joy, even if the path is a little rockier or a little more challenging. This commitment helps us step past feelings of responsibility and obligation and into a state of willingness.

We then take the power that we develop from self-love add it to the power we have over our internal reality. In doing so, we are able to transform our emotions and our thoughts to help and support us.

We can also direct this energy and power to our external reality and choose an environment and community that is supportive and loving. As a direct result, we create a loving internal and external world for ourselves, setting up environments where we can thrive without having to fight and without having to merely survive. This is how I have come to view self-love.

The Spoonful Analogy + Self-Love

If we go back to our spoonful analogy and consider what that looks like, we can see the steps to manifesting self-love—how we can translate this emotion, lifestyle, and idea into reality.

If a single spoonful of love that we share with the external world means basic human kindness, then consider self-love being three or more spoonfuls. When we utilize our words and actions in the spirit of self-love, we not only care for ourselves, but build an environment where we can live prosperously. It is then merely a matter of choosing the tools, words, and actions that resonate with us.

What Does It Mean to Love Yourself?

Before we get into some specifics about self-love, I ask that you take a moment to put what you've read to the test. Do you understand my understanding and perspective on self-love? Do you agree or need to modify my understanding? What will you do with this apple known as self-love?

What does it mean to love yourself? What does it look like? How does it feel?

Next, I would like you to take a moment to look within yourself. How would you classify your self-love? Is it a single drop, a babbling brook, or is it as vast and deep as the ocean? Is it based on conditions or is it unconditional?

Today, how strong and big is your self-love? Would you like it to become bigger?

As we've discussed, self-love is a choice. I encouraged you to love yourself with your first breath before we began our healing journey in Volume One. I asked that you not wait until you were the person you wanted to be, but that you choose to love yourself today merely because you are special.

The Power of Self-Love

I introduced self-love as the relationship we have with ourselves and illustrated how our self-love possesses the power to transform our lives. By taking a look at our understanding of love combined with our understanding of our internal and external reality, we will uncover the strength and power of self-love. It is important to remember that:

- We have influence only over the external world.
- Most relationships we have exist within the external world.
- Consequently, whether a relationship works and is healthy is not only dependent on what you do, but what the other person does, as well.
- We have complete control over our internal reality.
- Our relationship with ourselves exists within our internal reality.
- We have complete control over the healthiness and longevity of our self-love.

By taking a look at our understanding of our internal and external realities in conjunction with our relationships, we get to learn just how powerful our self-love can be. You don't need to wait for anybody or depend on anyone else in order to love yourself. Loving yourself can happen at any time and in any place, as long as you choose it.

But, like anything, you can't be expected to know something you have never been exposed to. If you've never learned about self-love or why it is so important and powerful, choose self-love today, right now. Rather than beating yourself up for not knowing something you've never learned, choose to display compassion for yourself.

Then, like any skill, piece of wisdom, or tool, choose to learn and seek out the knowledge you need to put the idea of self-love into practice.

Breathe in Self-Love

Before we break down the different elements of self-love and get into the tools we can utilize, take a moment to breathe with me. As we've learned during the course of this book, breathing deeply offers a myriad of benefits. Not only does deep breathing alter our mental state it can also be an act of conscious energy work. When we pair conscious energy work with self-love, we discover that self-love exists as a state of energy.

Like any emotion, self-love is not a substance we can see with our eyes, and yet it is as real as a book. In life we have many layers to our existence, one of which is what we can see, hear, taste, smell, and touch.

Another layer to our world is what we can't register with our five senses. This unseen or esoteric element to life can be hard to categorize and comprehend but every time we feel, think, or our intuition speaks to us, it shows itself.

When we combine the many layers of life, we can pull tools and wisdom to create a layered and more effective approach to life. This includes the insight we gain from our five senses, as well as practical skills, healthy wisdom, and esoteric truths like energy.

As we learned in Chapter Three, breathing deeply impacts our mental wellbeing as well as weaves us within the world. Each time we take a moment to breathe deeply we can also embrace ourselves as conscious energy workers.

As you set the timer for one minute, take this moment to consciously invite the energy of self-love into your body as you breathe in, and expel the stagnant energy of self-rejection as you breathe out.

Breathe in....

    Call on Spirit, your spirit guides, Mother Earth, and the Universe to send you the energy of self-love. Then, as your lungs expand, imagine this energy filling your body and traveling through your blood stream alongside this fresh oxygen.

Breathe out...

    As you push the air from your body, send any self-rejection, self-loathing, self-hate, or shame out with it. As this air leaves your body, ask your spirit guides to transmute this stagnant energy into new and revitalized love.

Take one minute to transform and create the reality that you love yourself. By consciously inviting and accepting the energy of self-love, you create on an esoteric level an environment that will support you as you learn and utilize the knowledge and tools of self-love that we will now cover.

Elements of Self-Love

Self-love has different elements that can aid us in the various areas of our lives. Since life is complex, self-love brings a level of depth that prepares and supports us on whatever leg of our life's journey we are on.

Perception: Self-Worth

The first shift that happens when we choose to develop a relationship with ourselves is that our perception changes. We saw within Volume One that our understanding of life can influence the quality and nature of our lives. The same can be said when we choose to love ourselves.

Through self-love, we begin to see the face in the mirror in a different way. The shift that we experience within our heart spreads to our mind and influences what we see. Through self-love, we can see ourselves as having worth and value.

As a result, when we see

- **Our selves:** We see worth and value. We are actively honoring our Special Truth.

- **Our dreams and desires:** They have value because we have value. If you remember meraki (creative love), this category of love is also a form of self-love. For each time we pursue a passion with devotion, creativity, and love we are not only immersed in meraki, but have demonstrated self-love.

- **Our obstacles:** They can be faced because we are worthy of success, and they can be overcome because we have strength and value that is greater than the fears and challenges.

- **The thoughts, opinions, emotions, and beliefs of others:** Hold less meaning and power when they clash with our knowledge that we are lovable and have value.

- **The actions and choices of others:** Will be understood in a different way. We will experience different thoughts, opinions, and beliefs in light of our self-love.

- **Our own actions and choices:** Will be utilized to pursue our dreams and path to healing and happiness. They will also be enacted from a place of love.

The Deserted Island Scenario

To achieve a greater understanding of the power and strength of self-love, consider this scenario:

One day you decide to go sightseeing. You rent a boat and head out to sea. Unfortunately, a great storm blows you far from shore and over the hours, the storm succeeds in transporting you to a deserted island. With a damaged boat, you are left to survive on your own until help can arrive.

With no one around, it's up to you to find the will to keep going. With no support team or cheerleaders, you must be able to say to yourself, "Come on, you can do it!"

Self-worth in this moment is necessary to push and sustain you as you learn through trial and error how to light a fire and build a shelter. So, here's the question…

If you were on a deserted island, would you be able to encourage yourself? Could you display compassion for yourself when your shelter falls apart? Would you feel as though you had a reason to keep going?

What you do on this deserted island until help arrives illustrates the power of self-love. Even when you are alone, there's still someone in your corner. Even when you make mistakes, you still experience acceptance and love. This is the strength and power we can discover from self-love.

So, if we can accomplish so much on a deserted island, what can we accomplish at home, with a support team and a host of resources?

Self-Worth vs. Flaws

Each of us has experienced life as a child. During that time we began to piece together the first version of our personal philosophy. At the same time, we were also living through various life experiences that left us wounded. These experiences provided us with false wisdom that we used to live our lives.

This created a domino effect. Our false wisdom led us to make unhealthy realizations and decisions, which in turn brought about more trauma and rotten apples. As a result, our false wisdom has left us with a need to put things to the test, to unlearn the lessons imparted to us during our survival, to unlearn the coping mechanisms of our youth, and to start on a healing journey to a better life.

Due to our hardships, we can be left with a core belief which also happens to be false wisdom. Due to our differences, weaknesses, and the imperfections of others, we're left asking, "What's wrong with me?" instead of, "What's happened to me?"

Self-worth can then be reasoned away by a wounded mind, one that doesn't allow you to justify your own value. So, if your wounded heart and mind is rebelling against me and the knowledge of self-love, you might just decline this apple of self-worth.

But before you say, "no thanks" to my apple— because I do want you to put what I say to the test—I have an argument for it.

Argument For Self-Worth

I would like you to consider someone you value in your life. This could be a friend, parent, partner, boss, or teacher. Think about this person. Why is it that you value them? Are they kind, loving, strong, smart?

Since you value this person, you accept that they have worth. Now, consider that person's weaknesses, flaws, and challenges. What was their last mistake? Have they done something that pushed your buttons? Have they shared with you their worries or fears?

Since we are all human beings and thus make mistakes, I think you'll find that despite this person's value, they have flaws and wounds. You've just walked me through the reasons they have worth. This example teaches us that people have value and worth even when they have weaknesses and flaws.

This argument for self-worth leaves me feeling absolutely positive that you have worth. You are special. You are lovable. No matter what flaws or weakness you have. No matter the mistakes you have made.

Shelf of Important Things

My mother shared with me this mental exercise to help your mind shift into a new perspective—a perspective where you see yourself as having value and worth. Give it a try...

Close your eyes and picture in your mind's eye a room filled with shelves. They line the wall and are placed within the middle of the room, just like a public library.

As you walk around this room, you find that on these shelves there are items—books, films, objects, and pictures. And as you continue to walk around this room, you discover that every item on these shelves holds special meaning to you. These items are symbols for the precious gifts, people, and moments of your life. You may not have these things currently, but in your mind's eye they exist on the shelf amongst all of your other important things.

Take some time to look around at:

- Pictures of people from your past and present. Or maybe a place, a childhood home or landscape.
- Films of different experiences, celebrations, and moments.
- Objects, like your favorite childhood toy or an item from a past dream or hobby. Maybe even a gift from Santa, or a family member, friend, or lover.

What did you find?

As you walk around the shelves displaying heartfelt moments of your life, consider just how lucky you have been. If you wish, express gratitude for that friend, moment, or object.

Before you return to the present moment, add one more item to your shelf. Place yourself onto the shelf, because you are important. You are precious.

Self-Care

As our self-love grows, it spreads from our hearts and into our minds, where we begin to see our own worth and value. Once our minds consider life from this new perspective, our self-love continues to spread and grow, this time reaching past our internal reality (heart and mind) and into the external reality.

Once in the external world, our self-love takes on the form of self-care. Self-care is our self-love put into action. It acts as a driving force for us to choose the places, people, and things that will be healthy for us and bring us joy. Self-care will also act as that deciding factor, initiating change even when challenges and obstacles try to stop us.

As we practice self-love, we will be living it through self-care, putting our actions, thoughts, and words towards happiness rather than tearing ourselves apart. I say *practice* because demonstrating self-love through every avenue of our lives is hard. To that end, we demonstrate self-love by practicing—not requiring ourselves to be perfect, but rather allowing ourselves to be who we are: human. Still learning and growing.

Self-Care Checklist

In a society where speed can be key, we can easily slip into poor habits that put ourselves at risk. As our life continues, we can become ungrounded and uncentered. Under these circumstances, we can stop expressing our self-love in the external world.

To get a better sense as to what level you display self-care, take a look at this checklist, where I list common symptoms of having low or no self-care.

Signs Your Level of Self-Care is Low:

Body:
- Restless body or muscle tension.
- Sleep deprivation or fatigue.
- Chronic illness.
- Loss of the connection with your body that manifests as over- or-under-eating, lack of awareness with regards to your pain or discomfort, or lack of awareness of the impact the foods and even drugs have on your wellbeing.

Mind:
- Consistent state of fear and anxiety/worry.
- Paranoia.
- Negative and self-sabotaging thoughts.
- Your mind is stuck running on a loop or feels like it's outside of your control.

Heart:
- Quick to anger or irritation.
- Consistent state of depression.
- Negative and self-sabotaging emotions/feelings.
- Feel like you're drowning in all your emotions.

Soul:
- Questioning the quality of life and the world.
- Unable to see the gift of human life.
- Feeling cursed or forever unlucky.

External Reality:
- Neglecting and harmful family and friends.
- Unbalanced state—spending too much time working or neglecting the things that bring you joy.
- In an environment where your thoughts are undervalued, or your feelings are not acknowledged and honored.

Having taken a look at these major signs of low self-care, which ones resonated with you? Which ones have you experienced in the past? As you gather insight into what areas of your life need improvement, choose self-compassion to guide you.

In order to heal, you need to know where you stand with yourself and where you stand with the world. How can you begin to heal and fix something if you don't know it's broken? Or that it is even broken at all?

Moving forward, as you practice self-care, choose to be patient and kind with yourself. You can't flip the switch and be totally balanced, healthy, and happy tomorrow. It's a process and some days will be better than others.

Self-care is more than placing a Band-Aid on a papercut. Self-care requires making decisions and choosing actions that are healthy and good for your body, mind, heart (emotions), and soul. Not only for today, but tomorrow as well.

Which is why we *practice* self-care.

In order for this book be accessible for each reader, I often times need to talk about things in broad terms or include only one or two examples. By taking the time to identify the areas of your life that need improvement, you can heal and thus exist in alignment with a Heart-Centered Life.

This personalized information, paired with the tools and wisdom you will learn, will help you to not only identify the wound, but identify the healing solution, as well. We can then continue on our healing journey by putting our growing self-love into action.

Sanctuary: An Act of Self-Care

I briefly touched on this idea of having a sanctuary here on Earth when we addressed conditional love. We discover the need for a sanctuary when we combine two known truths about life. The first truth is that we are a community, part of an ecosystem in which all life is linked together. As a result, others influence us and our lives. The second truth is that there are still wounded individuals in the world.

From these two known truths, we learn that other people and places possess the ability to endanger us, and so we need a sanctuary. When we build our sanctuary, we determine the quality of our environment, helping to ensure a life of prosperity.

Sanctuaries will act as our place on Earth where we can recover, find safety, heal, and enjoy happiness and love. A sanctuary most often times comes in the form of the home we find, build, and maintain for ourselves. But it can also be as small and simple as a bedroom or a quiet place in nature.

Not only is a sanctuary a wise and practical space in a world still healing and growing, but it is also an essential element of living a Heart-Centered Life. The choice to have a sanctuary is an act of self-love (self-care).

What is your sanctuary? If you haven't found one yet, what do you imagine it to look and feel like?

The Self-Love Oath

Building self-love can be difficult. This sometimes-foreign concept can be hard for us to latch onto. Since emotions can be difficult to define and understand, self-love can feel elusive.

With that in mind, I have created the self-love oath to get you started. As you build your self-love, your oath will grow and morph, becoming a unique representation of your self-love, designed in a way that is best for you.

The Self-Love Oath:
"I promise to love, honor, and cherish myself. To see myself through the eyes and heart of love. To accept my imperfections and quirks. To celebrate my good and bad days. To stand up for my needs and desires. I promise to practice self-love."

Chapter Seven Takeaways: Self-Love

- Self-love is the relationship we choose to have with ourselves.
- Since self-love is a choice; we step past need into a state of desire; from survival to a state of thriving.
- Self-love not only helps us in our life but also helps positively change the quality of human life here on Earth.
- Self-love changes how we understand and see ourselves (self-worth).
- Self-love also changes our choices and is translated into our external world (self-care).

CHAPTER 8

Self-Love In Action

ease this pain inside my heart
and let this river run its course

help me clear this message in me
and bring a new day, to help me try

for this is the reason why
we are given life

When I was a little girl, I struggled with needing to know what people thought about me and what they thought about life. I created a scenario where I was dependent on external sources to tell me of my worth. I felt that the actions and words of other people were messages about how they felt and what they thought of me, rather than who they were and what kind of a day they were having.

As a result, I placed my value in the hands of the external world and outside of my control. In doing so, I left myself open to moments of pain that could have otherwise been avoided.

What I love most about self-love is that it doesn't take a utopian society, a loving family, a fair government, or even money or status. Self-love only needs you—you deciding that you have worth. When we make this choice, we are saying, "I am worthy, I am lovable."

You can choose to love yourself today, and you can choose to start putting that love into action today. There is no need to wait until the stars align or for others to clue in. Like every other element we have addressed so far in our healing journey, you do not need to walk this path alone.

In the previous chapter we talked about what self-love is, why we want it in our lives, the impact our self-love has on our lives and the lives of others, and the different elements of self-love. With this understanding of self-love, we have reached the stage in our healing journey where we'll investigate some of the different ways in which we can put our self-love into action.

You will then be able to have tools and wisdom at your disposal to actively change your life, stepping into not only a thriving human experience, but an experience of love. You'll become that being of love living a Heart-Centered Life.

Self-Love: Heart

Love starts as a choice, an emotion that lives in our hearts, so that's where we begin. To reach this place in your heart and make a permanent home for your love, you first must choose this state of being. You must make a choice that you will spread your arms wide and open your heart to this emotion.

While our heart carries love, in truth, love is a state of being and an act of living. In my personal experience, love is the most vulnerable emotion there is and to choose a life of love is also a vulnerable act. But to understand just what this means, we first must remove the roadblocks and fears that we already carry with us. Because the sad truth is that the very meaning of this word, *vulnerability*, is incorrectly defined by society.

According to the Merriam Webster Dictionary, vulnerability is synonymous with defenselessness, susceptibility, and weakness. But we can't fault Webster's Dictionary for merely recording how society understands and feels about this word. Words, after all, are merely sounds that we as people have given specific meaning to.

No, the problem lies with how we have been taught to perceive and experience vulnerability. Can you think of what might have twisted the truth of vulnerability?

Yep, a seed of fear. Vulnerability when paired with a seed of fear conjures a very different experience as opposed to when vulnerability is paired with a seed of love. Due to the design and perpetuation of fear in our society, for many people, vulnerability is akin to suffering through an excruciating experience.

Many people know how important vulnerability is, and with that in mind, they put up with the painful experience. However, accepting this pain is not the answer. For those of us who live our lives with a seed of love, the experience and benefits—yes, benefits—that come from vulnerability have nothing to do with excruciating pain.

Vulnerability: The Healthy Truth

Earlier in this book, I introduced you to research-storyteller, Brené Brown PH.D., LMSW, to help explain conditional love and the different elements to trust. Not only has she uncovered the various elements to trust but she had spent over seventeen years studying shame and, by extension, vulnerability.

Her groundbreaking work is worth looking into. Whether it's her TED Talks or her books, the knowledge she shares will help you improve the quality of your life. She has discovered, through years of research, the healthy truth behind what vulnerability is and why we need it.

Through my healing journey, Brené Brown's work was introduced to me by my mom. Not only was Brown's research enlightening, but I took her knowledge on vulnerability and viewed it first from the lens of a seed of fear, then from the lens of a seed of love.

Vulnerability and a Seed of Fear

What I discovered through my own contemplation is that when vulnerability is paired with a seed of fear, it taints the experience. People who live their lives from this state of fear live with the false message that they are not worthy.

The impact of this false message is not only harmful to the individual but to our community as a whole. For when we fail to see our own worth, we feel shame, guilt, and disgust with ourselves. We come away thinking that we are un-lovable and act accordingly, separating ourselves from others.

This separation is a good thing, according to a fear-based leadership, because it divides the people. It keeps our community stuck merely existing on a spiritual soul level, blocking it from reaching a conscious level and a conscious way of living.

Due to the impact of fear, we can see how people experience vulnerability as an excruciating ordeal that demands we open up and let all our faults and shames be seen.

Vulnerability and a Seed of Love

When we look at vulnerability through the lens of fear, it can be easy to walk away with the mistaken belief (rotten apple) that vulnerability is weakness. But as one who lives life based on a seed of love, I can honestly say that how I experience vulnerability is worlds apart from how fear would have us see, experience, and know vulnerability.

You might not look at yourself as being lovable and worthy today, not because this is an objective truth, but because you have rotten apples that have separated you from yourself. Before we can put our self-love into action, starting with our heart, we need to purge the rotten apples that block us from living lives filled with love.

It is time to leave the fear that you're not worthy of connection on the ground with all the other rotten apples. As Brené Brown says in her *The Power of Vulnerability* TED Talk, "Connection is why we're here. It gives purpose and meaning to our lives. This is what it's all about." And it's not just connection with each other, but connection with ourselves.

Each time we choose to love someone, we are inviting them into our lives and also into our internal reality. Each time we dare to dream, we are opening ourselves up to things not yet created. Each time we choose to engage with ourselves, with the world, and with life, we are displaying vulnerability.

So, what is the healthy truth of vulnerability?

VULNERABILITY:

"Our most accurate measurement of courage."

~Brené Brown PH.D., LMSW from TED Talk: *Listening to Shame*

COURAGE:

"Tell the story of who you are with your whole heart."

~Brené Brown PH.D., LMSW from TED Talk: *The Power of Vulnerability*

Here's the truth of things: vulnerability is not weakness. According to Brown, vulnerability is "the birthplace of innovation, creativity, and change." (Brené Brown PH.D., LMSW Ted Talk: *Listening to Shame*)

If we consider for a moment the truth of a loving Spirit, then we learn that something as fundamentally necessary for human connection, like vulnerability, would not be designed to be painful.

Yes, there is risk and exposure when we open up ourselves to:
- The truth of who we are.
- Others.
- The truth of who others are.
- Dreams and hopes.

But these experiences do not come with the mandatory prerequisite of pain. Vulnerability is choosing to open our arms to ourselves and to the world in a wise and healthy manner (think about that conditional love). By choosing to be open to yourself, you remove the blocks from your heart, and love stops being an idea and becomes the truth. Love becomes real, and we become beings of love.

Dynamic Emotions

Now that we understand the truth of vulnerability and have opened our arms wide to the love we have to experience and share, let's dig into different ways we can put our love into action, for as I said, love is a state of being and an act of living.

When we see love as an action, we learn that the emotions we feel have worth and value simply because *we* have worth and value. By choosing a thriving human experience with a seed of love, we not only stop surviving and begin thriving, but we also reach an environment where all of who we are is honored.

Once we stop living a life of survival and fear, we feel safe to experience, address, and honor our emotions. This opens us up to all the emotions that have been hidden in the background but have been influencing our life just the same. As a result, we begin to experience a dynamic array of sensations.

Rather than being just happy or scared, we uncover a concoction of emotions. Remember how I felt so many different things when I gave my first public speech? Well, when we start honoring every part of ourselves, all of our emotions are able to come to the surface and be heard.

Choosing to honor all your emotions in your heart is an act of self-love. Not only that, but there are a myriad of benefits to living your live with dynamic emotions:

- You become aware of your feelings. This enables you to trace back your actions to their emotional root cause and uncover wounds needing healing, rotten apples needing purging, and a greater understanding of yourself.

- Not only does this help facilitate change, but by connecting with how you feel and how and why you feel that way, you influence your life, developing a deeper relationship with yourself—one that's built with self-love.

- The life you live becomes fuller. You consciously feel more in the moment now that your emotions can shine.

- You learn to be more compassionate and forgiving towards others, because you yourself feel a lot, too.

- It's easier to be kind because your emotional response to a situation becomes stronger.

While not all cultures and societies are supportive in allowing all of your feelings to be a part of your life, by choosing to honor how you feel, you are choosing to love all of yourself. This choice not only means you are living the life of your dreams, but that you are changing our collective culture and community simply by healing.

Emotions: Going from Marching to Dancing.

As you begin to listen to and honor how you feel, it is common to start living a more dynamic life. I equate this transition with the analogy of marching and then dancing.

When we're in survival mode, our conscious knowledge is limited to a single emotion (fear, anger, happy, love = bad or good). Since we're too busy trying to survive, we don't have time for all we feel. It's as if we are marching, consistently moving in the same direction with the same actions and speed.

But as we begin to transform, more of what we feel will come to the surface. As a result, we will no longer live our lives in this same monotone fashion. We will begin to dance. Our morning might stink, but we can choose to move on, and the day may end completely differently than how it started. From moment to moment, we are able to shift, reflecting the emotions we feel.

Though this is not only natural but healthy, I have found that in my society and with people I'm getting to know, my fluctuation in emotions and subsequent actions can be met with shock. To complicate matters, this shock can leave people feeling uncomfortable or unsafe, which has the potential to create rotten apples that can be passed down throughout generations.

So, despite the rotten apples that tell you you're "overly emotional," or "too sensitive," know the truth: that you are loving and honoring your feelings, because your feelings matter, because you matter.

Dynamic Emotions and Fear

We are on a path where our wounded being is healing and we are transforming the world in which we live so that we can reduce the pain and increase the happiness we experience. This elevation to a thriving experience doesn't mean we will suddenly live a life free of fear. Fear is still a human emotion. So, what *does* it mean?

It means that fear will no longer be constant. That when it does pop up (some experiences are honestly, necessarily frightening), we will possess the skills, tools, and healthy understanding to address our fear in a healthy way.

We will be able to honor the fear and then let the moment and all corresponding emotions go. Those emotions will settle in the past and our next moment will hold the potential for love, healing, and happiness, because we have built our life and world around love.

Due to the copious amounts of fear in our lives, chances are that our relationship with fear is currently unhealthy, but it doesn't need to stay that way. Fear and other painful emotions are not something we must avoid or worry about experiencing.

Fear, when healthy, communicates to us and others:
- The importance of a situation.
- An inexperience or lack of knowledge.
- A past experience that caused a wound.
- Evidence that we need change and healing in our culture.
- Evidence that a part of our human life is not being honored or is endangered.
- Evidence that a wounded person is threatening our community.

Allow the emotion to teach you about the situation and/or person; allow it to guide you. While it's not an emotion I seek, I have experienced fear since living a Heart-Centered Life. It's ok to be scared.

The "Good" and the "Bad"
While there are definitely some emotions that we want to experience as often as possible (love and happiness), and there are others we would like to avoid (fear and grief), both are a part of the human condition.

If we were to deny ourselves the right to feel the pain, we would be denying ourselves the right to be human. So, while there are emotions we define as "good" and "bad," it is important to honor them all.

Not only does honoring your emotions become an act of love, but we can't select what emotions we feel. When we cut ourselves off from the pain, we are in essence cutting ourselves off from our heart, which is also the home of hope, love, and forgiveness.

Who we are includes the happy and the sad moments. Living a life of love means supporting your heart and embracing your emotions and feelings, the good, the bad, and the in-between.

Self-Worth: Mind

When we develop a relationship with ourselves, we begin by feeling love in our hearts. It then spreads to our minds. When this happens, our very perception of our worth and of the world changes. Some of this change happens subconsciously where how we hear, understand, and respond to the external world shifts. Other times, it takes a conscious choice to change our perception. We may even need to learn new tools, wisdom, and skills to translate our self-love into a new mental state.

So, when a bully attempts to tell you your worth, you no longer feel any truth to their words. Due to your healing you not only feel but know that you are worthy and loveable. When a new opportunity presents itself, you can see it working out in your favor; you can see yourself getting that job or promotion or going on that life-changing adventure.

Self-Talk

Within our mind we store the wisdom, philosophy, perception, and data that we have collected and created throughout our lives. Together, these pieces structure our mind and our quality of life. Another element that exists within our mind is our inner dialogue or our self-talk.

In our mind, we have a series of voices and thoughts that, when left unsupervised, can create pain. One voice comes from our heart and soul. This true voice of ours loves and supports us. But sadly, due to that seed of fear, there is another voice that disguises itself. It sounds just like you, but instead of supporting you, it verbalizes all of your worst fears and concerns, and utilizes rotten apples that create harm and doubt within your mind.

This dysfunctional voice becomes even more potent when we choose to focus on the scarcity in our life. Our mind then accommodates this perception and when we look out into the world or even in a mirror, all that doesn't fall into this category gets filtered out. We become blind to things likes abundance, health, love, and happiness.

In Canada, at Queen's University, Julie Tseng and Jordan Poppenk conducted a study titled, "Brain meta-state transitions demarcate thoughts across task contexts exposing the mental noise of trait neuroticism." Their study uncovered that the average human has on average 6,200 thoughts per day.

This research shows us just how important our thoughts are. Through redundancy and repetition, the impact of the quality of our thought is great. Ginormous. As water carves canyons and polishes stone, thoughts do the same.

Positively or negatively, for better or for worse, our thoughts impact our lives, our decisions, opinions, personality traits, and self-worth. As we manifest change within our lives, we need to change our thoughts, as well. Instead of letting the dysfunctional voices in our head have free reign, we must give the power over to our true voice to create thoughts that will unlock doors and remove obstacles.

Often times, we are so disconnected from ourselves that we don't even realize we have self-talk, nor are we aware of what that talk might be saying. Think of a river as it runs along its path. The river has the ability to mold, cut, shape and polish giant stone. Not through the force of the water, but by the repetitiveness of its flowing.

When we hear a bully tell us lies about ourselves, we can ignore him or her. But should the bully choose to be like the river and tell us lies about ourselves every day, by the end of the year, we just might begin to believe them—unless we have an inner dialogue that points out that happy people don't act that way, and that we are worthy.

As you get in touch with yourself, you might not like what you find. What kind of toxic thoughts are running through your head? How are they impacting your life? Through building self-worth, we can begin to transform our self-talk from rotten apples to healthy wisdom.

Affirmations

One of the ways we can rewrite the dialogue of our inner voice is through the tool known as affirmations. Affirmations are positive phrases we think or say to ourselves to change our thought patterns and thus our reality. They're a great way to bring about change because they alter our outlook, and they can act as a prayer.

Like that bully who tells you lies, affirmations can be like a river and carve away the false wisdom that lives in your head. Through repetition you can not only adopt a new perception but actively replace your negative self-talk, rather than just hoping things will get better.

Creating Affirmations

Affirmations can be created by anyone, for anything. They are merely phrases or sentences meant to communicate our worth, our safety, and our potential, to change how we see and even how we feel about life.

Some guidelines include:
- Affirmations are always in the present tense.
- Affirmations are positive.
  - Instead of "Bad things are going away," we say, "Good things are manifesting."

Thus, your focus is on the abundance entering your life.

Where to put your affirmations:
- Write them on sticky-notes or pieces of paper.
- Leave them in your wallet or purse.
- Place them on your mirror in your bathroom.
- Use them as a bookmark.

- Place them on the inside of a kitchen cabinet.
- Place them on your dashboard (just don't let them distract you from your driving).
- Place them near your computer.
- Place them on your desk.
- Place them where you will see them or where the affirmation will apply.

Examples of Affirmations:
- "I love myself."
- "I choose to love myself in my entirety."
- "I demonstrate self-love daily."
- "I choose to make healthy decisions to shape my reality into one of happiness."

Getting Started:
I know that when I first started saying affirmations to myself, I felt awkward. Repeating the same small phrase over and over was monotonous. Affirmations are a tool requiring dedication and consistency. We will only experience results if we stick with the affirmation rather than saying it just once and expecting everything to magically be all better.

While they lack the glamour other tools have, affirmations are extremely effective when we utilize them with regularity. Whether you start with a simple affirmation like, "I love myself," or, "I am worthy," or get more specific, like, "I feel good and it is safe to feel good," you can design a number of affirmations that resonate with you. Affirmations will help you carve away the false wisdom and instill within your inner voice a strength that comes straight from your heart.

Perception and Mundane Acts

When we choose to love, our perception changes, but it can still get caught on old thought patterns and habits. These outdated methods of perception can challenge the efficacy of our Heart-Centered lifestyle until we replace them. We can practice being present while rewriting our inner dialogue by taking the time to re-approach daily activities.

Whether they're dishes, groceries, laundry, or even teeth brushing, we might be mis-perceiving the things we do on a daily or weekly basis. Our perception of our daily tasks matters because, as we've seen, our perception determines our experience.

While doing the dishes might not be my favorite task, my understanding of the task determines what emotions I will feel when I perform it, as well as how much effort it will require of me. When I see dishes through the eyes of fear, I see them as:

- Boring.
- Annoying.
- Messy.
- Not the way I want to spend my time.

But when seen through the eyes of love, I come to know them as being an avenue to healthy food, a friendly environment, and a gift. When we love ourselves, the food we put into our body matters. The time we spend with family matters.

We can choose to see doing the dishes as a gift. As a reflection of the healthy and tasty food we eat, the family we love, and the physical body that is healthy and can stand up and wash them. Sure, they may never be my favorite chore (I much prefer cooking), but I know that dirty dishes represent the things that I not only want, but love.

Be it the dishes or the laundry, how we understand the different, mundane elements of our life determines how we will experience them. My mom loves to say, "It's not the event but how you perceive it."

As you practice being in the present moment you will be able to consider how you perceive and address mundane moments like cooking or cleaning. For when we acknowledge that our inner dialogue shapes our perception and experience, we become empowered to change the very nature of our daily lives.

If I love Myself?

As you consider what it means to clean, cook, exercise, etc., utilize this question to help you navigate to a healthy perception. If you love yourself (which is what we're practicing) what value is there to cooking? If you love yourself, would you postpone a necessary appointment or get it promptly taken care of?

If you love yourself....
- What would you do?
- When would you do it?
- How would you feel and perceive _____?

> **Taking it another step further: "If I Love?"**
>
> The question, "If I loved myself…" can help us navigate through the choices, actions, decisions, and perceptions we utilize in our personal life. We can take this a step further with the question, "If I love…"
>
> With this question, we can navigate how we would treat those in the external world. As a being of love, what would you do? What would you say? This question can help guide you as you work to display unconditional love to the world around you.

Developing Self-Love and Self-Worth

Putting our self-love into action takes on many forms and comes with numerous tools so that we can not only love every aspect of ourselves but choose tools that resonate with us. While affirmations work to re-wire our inner voice, some tools work not only with regard to our hearts, but our minds, as well. Here are some more ways we can put our self-love into action.

Self-Knowledge

Self-love means choosing to have a relationship with ourselves. One of the ways we can put this idea into action is by taking the time to connect with ourselves. This connection can mean tuning into our inner dialogue. It can also mean taking the time to listen to our hearts to discover our dreams.

Not only will this self-knowledge help you design a personal, thriving human experience by offering insight into what you want out of life, but it will also help shed light on your darkness. You will not only love yourself, but achieve an authentic love. You will be able to see all of who you are and embrace it all.

You will not only know how you feel and what you think, but you will be in a position to see your full, true self, and with that love forgive. You'll achieve another layer of healing as you move forward with your life.

This healing will help you to release old guilt or sorrow so that it can return to the past, and stop tainting the present moment with old pain and dysfunction. You will then be in a position to identify areas that need growth and improvement for your next layer of healing.

Self-Knowledge Will Answer These Questions:
- Who are you?
- What do you believe in?
- What do you value?
- What's your code?
- What's your character?
- What do you like/love?
- What do you dislike?
- What do you want, desire, and dream of?

Journaling:

Taking the time to turn around and face ourselves, to travel through the darkness and carry ourselves back into the light, not only requires courage, but acceptance. Being open to who you are and not what you imagine can be nerve-racking—especially when we've lost touch with ourselves.

I understand that there might be aspects about ourselves that we don't wish to see, or that we wish were different, so now is your chance. It's time to make the changes in your life that will lead you to your happiness. But before we make changes, we need to know who we are.

In order to do that, we need to train our body to check-in with itself. As we create this healthy habit, it will become a natural occurrence in our life. Not only will it help us to identify rotten apples, but it will also help our own mind and heart to know that we are not alone.

One technique to get in tune with ourselves is journaling. The purpose of journaling is to give voice to your inner dialogue, your feelings, the conscious and subconscious parts of yourself.

What is Journaling?

Now, I understand that the word "journaling" can elicit different thoughts, feelings, and images. We might think of a scene from a movie where the girl pours her heart out to her diary. We might imagine sharing feelings and experience an uncomfortable sensation settling inside of us. Which is why we might think, "Nope." But journaling, just like anything else in life, is what you choose to make of it. It's your perception of reality.

Speaking personally, I don't do the whole, "This is what happened today; I feel," or even the "Dear Diary" salutations. I have never been successful in emulating the scenes from the movies, but this doesn't mean I don't journal. I merely made this wonderful tool work for me.

Journaling is a tool that I want you to enjoy, so make it work for you.

CHAPTER 8: SELF-LOVE IN ACTION

Journaling is meant to help you reconnect with yourself. You can achieve this through traditional journaling: writing at a desk in full sentences or filling out writing prompts. As for myself, writing traditionally is not how I am most effective. Instead, I found what works best for me is writing poetry.

Through this free form, I am able to harness all those muddled emotions and thoughts from within me and release them out into the world. To this day, I fill notebooks with poems. Some I love and share with others, and others I keep private, for my eyes alone.

At the start of each chapter and each section within Volume One, I have included a poem that I have written. Some of them date back to high school; others I wrote while I wrote this book.

In my personal experience, I can give voice to my inner thoughts, feelings, and my subconscious when I write poetry. If you choose to utilize journaling as a tool for self-discovery, try out different methods of writing to find what works for you.

Whether your journaling takes on the form of poetry, letters, or prose, this tool of self-discovery will help you dig into every area of your life. When you do, you can uncover habits, thoughts, feelings, or patterns you were not familiar with. You will then be equipped with the self-knowledge you need in order to make the changes you desire. From there, the healing, discoveries, and achievements are limitless.

Self-Care: External World

While I categorize the process of developing self-love as a feeling (heart), a perception (mind; self-worth), and then as an external manifestation within the external world (self-care), in truth, these various elements of self-love happen simultaneously. That being said, once we feel and perceive ourselves from this place of self-love, we begin to naturally, and even subconsciously, change into beings of love.

As a direct result, our perception of life shifts, and this change alters who we are and what we do in the external world. While we can put self-care techniques in place, the transformation that occurs within us naturally leads to self-care in the external world.

When we start to see ourselves as having worth, the way we carry ourselves changes. With self-compassion, we stop having total meltdowns when human error (a part of the human condition) happens. We also change what we say and who we talk to in order to reflect our value, needs, and desires.

We can aid our own transformation when we choose to learn about self-care techniques, healthy behaviors, and tools that will either help remove the dysfunction from our lives or help us operate in the world from a new and healthy place. Here are just a few things that will change when you carry the truth that you are loved and cherished within you.

Self-Advocacy

When we lack the information that we matter, we can fall into all kinds of unhealthy lifestyles and habits. But when we return our worth into our own hands and choose self-love, we can naturally remedy many of our unhealthy habits. One of the changes that transpires is that we stop waiting.

Rather than waiting for someone else to wake up to your wonderfulness, your needs, or even to your civil liberties, take this truth into your own hands. It's time to learn to self-advocate.

CHAPTER 8: SELF-LOVE IN ACTION

> **SELF-ADVOCACY:**
> The ability to express your needs, wants, thoughts and feelings. To know your rights and responsibilities and to take accountability for your responsibility and use it to pursue what you desire.

Self-advocacy is a wonderful tool because we can apply it to every facet of our lives. When we self-advocate, we put our self-love and worth into action. We give voice to our needs and wants; we stop waiting.

Whether we choose to say "no" to pain and hardship and "yes" to opportunities, or we choose to walk away from dysfunction and towards our dreams, self-advocacy allows us to embrace our power. To not just wish on a star but to put into place the plans to manifest our wishes. This doesn't mean we walk the path alone; it merely means that we support ourselves and are on our own side, just like our healthy friends and family are.

Examples of Lacking Self-Advocacy

- We rely on the external world for validation and worth. Not only does this put our worth into the hands of others, but it can also trigger mania (the 10th category of love). In addition, our need for worth taints all human connection and interaction because we're busy trying to feel loved and worthy and to keep that feeling.

- We can display co-dependent behavior and act like a doormat. When we're co-dependent, we can either release control of our lives or take on control of other people's lives. In either case, this false perception about who is responsible for our happiness and life not only creates unattainable standards, but it can leave your voice unheard.

- With a misperceived need for love from others we can view other people's happiness as our responsibility. We do this in an effort to keep that love. But in doing so we create standards that we can't meet. A perfect recipe for failure since each person is responsible their individual happiness.

Why We Need Self-Advocacy

When we are under the mistaken belief that we can't say "no" to those we love or even to our superiors, it can become a challenge to self-advocate. When we self-advocate, we not only change the nature of our relationships, we also disrupt, and potentially end, our dysfunctional connections with others.

That's why self-advocacy can feel foreign and hard. It's made all the more difficult when others refuse to display respect towards us. These challenges can test us. Due to these circumstances, I would like you to consider this new apple, and my argument for self-advocacy.

Conclusion

Self-advocacy is a necessary component to a healthy life.

Argument One

How you treat yourself communicates to others your own perceived value of self.

When we permit others:
- To speak rudely;
- To demand perfection;
- To make us responsible for their lives and happiness;
- To order us about, or
- To abuse us physically or verbally,

we are communicating to them. We are telling them through our non-action or our compliance that what they've done is ok. While I would love every human being on the planet to display basic human kindness and respect, it is not someone else's responsibility to know better.

Therefore, when you choose to say, "no," "please stop," or use your feet to walk away and in challenging cases call for help, you are communicating, through your words and actions, that you need to be treated with basic human kindness and respect. As a result, you change how you experience life and the culture around you.

This change not only puts your self-love into action, but it sends out a ripple that can inspire others and change the kind of world we all live in.

Argument Two

When we choose to self-advocate, we honor the truth of responsibility and our unalienable rights. In America's Declaration of Independence, our forefathers defined that among our unalienable rights is "Life, Liberty, and the pursuit of Happiness." When you combine our rights with the responsibility we have for our own lives, we discover that self-advocacy honors these truths.

With this insight into self-advocacy, consider this new apple. Do you agree with me that self-advocacy is a necessary element to living a healthy life?

Examples of Self-Advocacy:
- Saying "no," or "please stop" when others treat you poorly.
- Saying "yes" to opportunities and the various things we desire.
- Using our actions to walk away or towards things, depending on our desires and their healthiness.
- Saying "no" to the responsibilities and situations that are not ours or do not serve us.
- Saying "no" to things that are not healthy for you, such as extra work, unhealthy foods, or even unhealthy people, places, and activities.

While self-advocacy is a natural part of a healthy life, it is also a learned skill. So, avoid that assumption trap and choose to forgive yourself for not knowing something you have never been taught, exposed to, or learned. Instead, choose to practice self-love through self-compassion and self-forgiveness.

As you develop your skills in self-advocacy, I also challenge you to consider how you are standing up for yourself. Can you communicate "no" in a kind and polite manner? Can you choose actions and words that not only advocate for you but also display the quality of character that you desire? While you are self-advocating, can you also respect others as they do the same?

Self-Advocacy and Vulnerability

Self-advocacy teaches us to say "no" to harm and "yes" to opportunities, but I have recently discovered that, like all things, too much is just as bad as too little. While self-advocacy is a form of self-worth and self-care, where we communicate to the external world that we matter, it can be taken too far.

Not all people are taught that they can choose who and what is in their lives, ensuring that their life remains safe and happy.

Learning this skill takes practice and it can be especially hard to draw the line when it is to the displeasure of those we love.

However, as I said earlier, too much can be just as harmful as too little. When we begin to live our lives looking out for ourselves not only in our internal world, but in our external world as well, we can get pretty good at saying "no" to those we call friends and family.

But if we go too far, this wisdom of self-care can become a detriment and turn sour, transforming our apple into a rotten state. For when we take self-advocacy too far, we can create a sense of logic that closes us off from the world. We can lose touch with compassion and the love in our own heart.

Self-Advocacy Taken Too Far

When we take self-advocacy too far, our perspective narrows and we experience tunnel vision, where our needs and rights surpass everyone else's. In this extreme version of self-advocacy, we can lose sight of other's rights and needs. We can also lose compassion and our words and actions can turn harsh, demanding, and egotistical, where we expect and even demand life to be our way. When we acknowledge the Special Truth, we are not only acknowledging our own worth, but the worth of every other human being.

Sometimes, depending on the situation, you'll need to compromise or even concede, because just as you are special, and advocating for yourself is important, life on Earth doesn't always leave us with the end result we desire (like that job or partner). Yet, I have found that when we work with the flow and rhythm of life, things always work out as they are meant to.

In addition, when we take self-advocacy too far, we can create a series of logical thought that jeopardizes our healthy lifestyle:
1. I advocate for myself; this is an act of self-love.
2. X has done Y, which is not healthy for me.
3. To demonstrate self-care, I will
    - Cut this person out of my life.
    - Shut down emotionally.
    - Question if I will ever let them back in.

When we take this series of logic too far, we close off our hearts. We then aren't living a prosperous life; this is where vulnerability comes in.

Determining Who Gets Invited Back in and Who Gets Let Go

I would love to tell you that if we simply cut out the people, places, and things that have harmed us, we will discover our thriving human experience, but in actuality, if we do these things, we lose the chance for a life of prosperity.

We all make mistakes. We all have chosen, at one time or another, a path that has harmed others and even ourselves. We are human beings and part of the human condition is human error. So, what is the answer? The answer is balance.

I have found a wonderful life when I invite people, places, and things into my world (vulnerability). When I honor my connection with the world, I weave myself with life and into my thriving human experience.

But there are also a lot of smart reasons to say "no." Safety is not a joke. So, how do you let those who have hurt you back in? Who gets another chance and to whom do you say "no"? After all, some people are dangerous and it is unwise to let them back in.

CHAPTER 8: SELF-LOVE IN ACTION

Listen to your heart and your head; let them guide you in tandem. You're the only one who knows the person, the situation, the harm you've sustained, and your own strength.

Consideration One: Harm

What wound did you sustain? Was it mental, emotional, physical? What was the level of harm: small, medium, or large? Who or what harmed you?

Consideration Two: Context

Person: Who are they?

Is this normal behavior or were they having a bad day? The hurt you feel is real, and your course of action must not only honor how you feel but acknowledge the severity of the situation.

If this person doesn't normally cause harm or doesn't understand that what they said or did hurt you, then communicate your feelings. Through communication, you can strengthen the bonds and quality of your relationship.

Sometimes, the situation goes all the way back to that assumed knowledge. When we encounter rude and hurtful acts, we perceive them to be accurate communication—that this person is telling me that they don't respect me as a person. That they fail to see my worth.

We assume they know that their words are rude and hurtful. This assumption is typically correct—most people know the basics to kindness and respect, but not everyone does. From their perspective, they see no problem or harm connected to their actions or word choice. For this reason, communication is key.

Consider talking with this person and saying, "When you did Y, my feelings got hurt. Did you know that when you do/say Y that you're being rude and disrespectful?"

Sometimes, the conversations that start out awkwardly lead to deeper connection. You give the other person the opportunity to learn something they didn't know before. And now, you both know the truth of the situation from both sides, because you each matter.

When we jump to conclusions, we stop living the life of kindness and consideration that we seek (unconditional love). However, if this isn't the first time that someone chose not to listen when you tell them they've hurt you, or if these hurtful manners, words, and actions are part of their personality, it's time to seriously consider if it is still an act of self-love to stay in the relationship. Maybe it's time to walk away.

Situation: Where were you or what were you doing?

Is this typical behavior or out of the ordinary? What sort of environment is being supported and cultivated? Is this environment healthy and safe? If it is typically destructive behavior, it might be time to walk away.

Consideration Three: Strength of Your Heart

When your heart feels strong enough or even when it doesn't feel 100%, let those who try to be kind back in. When your head speaks truth—that this person is so deep into a life lesson that they are lost and wounded—separate yourself to remain safe.

At the end of the day, you are the one who knows the specifics of a situation. You can talk with a trusted friend to navigate the situation so that you remain a vulnerable but practical person.

If you feel it's safe, talk to the person who hurt you and communicate how you feel. If their response is apologetic and they make efforts to fix the problem, then they are communicating through their words and actions the great quality of who they are.

On the other hand, if they don't care or make no efforts to change, even if they said they will, they are again communicating their quality of character. Which will inform you that it's time to walk away and continue towards your happy life.

Boundaries

A form of self-advocacy, boundaries help us to maintain a healthy lifestyle and environment. They help us to determine who and what we weave into our life.

> PERSONAL BOUNDARIES:
> The guidelines and limits that we create to identify the health and personal preferences we have for how people treat and behave towards us.

We can use boundaries to protect our mental, emotional, physical, and spiritual wellbeing. They protect us from manipulation, violation, harm, and pain. They also communicate our self-respect, self-love, and health.

Why We Need Boundaries
When we lack boundaries, we can confuse our needs and wants with the needs and wants of others, at times creating an environment primed for a co-dependent relationship. By creating personal boundaries, we honor our need for privacy, personal space, and even what it is we want from life. At the same time, we help to create a more harmonious environment around us.

We achieve this harmony by building and maintaining healthy boundaries. At first there might be some push-back, as boundaries can change the dynamics of our relationships. We might even lose some friends who are not interested in healing but remember that boundaries are an important element to a healthy lifestyle built with trust.

In the end, boundaries help create an environment where our space and personality are respected and honored. When we honor our boundaries, we eliminate potentially painful, argumentative, unwanted, and unhealthy moments from our present and future.

Creating Personal Boundaries

Since boundaries apply to every area of life, they can look different based on the situation, who it involves, and even from person to person. We are individuals with different needs and wants. As a result, we create boundaries based on conclusions, wisdom (apples), opinions, personal preference, past experiences, and even social and cultural norms.

Due to our individualism, our preferences when creating boundaries and the strictness with which we support those boundaries varies. For example, I love to hug people. So my personal physical boundaries are pretty small, only really showing themselves around strangers and those who give off a creepy vibe. But another person might not want to be touched at all, even by loved ones.

Our boundaries reflect who we are, as well as our surroundings. As I said, my physical boundaries when it comes to loved ones are pretty non-existent, but they are strong and enforced around strangers.

Step One: Identify your needs and wants.

Through self-discovery we gain insight not only into our personality but into what we value, and what we envision and dream for our life. This knowledge helps us to navigate our life.

Step Two: Adopt the apple that personal boundaries are important and are an act of self-care.

By accepting this new apple on boundaries, this additional piece of wisdom gets added to our personal philosophy. From there, it is no longer just a piece of wisdom, but a perception that leads to self-love in action.

Step Three: Communicate your needs and wants.

While all people need boundaries, as we've seen, boundaries are influenced by who we are. To that end, we must communicate our specific preferences to those around us.

How am I to know you don't like hugs unless you tell me? How are you to know that I need some space to recharge unless I tell you?

Step Four: Monitor and maintain your boundaries.

When we are first creating boundaries, or at the start of a new relationship, we need to communicate our needs and wants. Hopefully afterwards, those around us will learn to respect our boundaries, only needing kind reminders. If someone chooses to ignore these boundaries, it is a clear sign of dysfunctional behavior, and they might not be a person with whom you wish to continue a relationship.

Once we've created and communicated our boundaries, we only need to monitor and maintain them.

Step Five: Remember that this is a practice.

Boundaries are an act of self-care. They are also a learned skill. So, whether you've been using boundaries or are just learning, choose to continue this theme of self-care and give yourself time, patience, and compassion.

Step Six: Honor other's personal boundaries.

When we acknowledge the Special Truth, we discover our own value. We also discover the value of every other person. As you enforce and advocate for your boundaries, pay attention to other people's boundaries and choose to honor them as well.

Respecting boundaries honors the Golden Rule (treat others the way you wish to be treated) and demonstrates love and respect, and that you are a person of good quality and character. When you're unclear about someone else's boundaries, ask—use the tool of communication.

Examples of Boundaries

- **Physical:** Choosing when people can step into our space or touch us. Choosing who and when people can enter our home, room, and look through our things.

- **Emotional:** Choosing what we share with regard to our feelings or even what we have going on in our lives.

- **Mental:** Choosing which apples we select about life, love, success, etc., as well as how we will experience a moment. Choosing our opinion on a subject and what we value.

- **Spiritual:** Choosing what to believe and what we share about our beliefs. Even choosing whether or not to enter into a debate about the reality of life and how it all works.

- **Personality:** Honoring who we want to be as people, what we desire from life, and how we present ourselves to the world. This way, when we make decisions about our careers or families, it reflects our individual dreams and not someone else's.

- **Time:** Choosing how we utilize our days and how much time another person has in our company.

- **Material Goods:** Choosing with whom we share our things and to whom we loan money.

Boundaries communicate to the world our understanding of our worth, who we are, and how we plan on living our lives. Through communication and conditional love, we can create internal and external environments that embody the philosophies of love, healing, and happiness.

Shadow Work

When I entered the 6th grade, I entered into a new world that brought with it new experiences, challenges, and a new best friend. Along with these new elements, I uncovered a truth about myself I had not known before.

Uncovering this truth was unpleasant and it would take me a number of years before I would change paths and break free of this rotten apple. When I look back, I not only present myself with an opportunity for compassion and self-forgiveness, but I learn more, as well.

These past few days, my mind has been taking trips down memory lane. With the big accomplishment of my first book being published, I have been looking back at how it all started. Through reflection I have been able to review that time in my life as a full picture. As a direct result, new truths have come to light.

When I first discovered that I cared about what others thought I was not only shocked, but I continued down a path that put social acceptance and the pleasing of others before my own truths.

In retrospect, I am at peace with the decisions I made in my youth, but with wiser eyes, I can see the mistake I made when I continued down that path rather than testing my rotten apple and promptly changing course.

When I first entered the sixth grade I was met with resistance to my particular brand of uniqueness. Due to this I experienced the social and emotional environment of one who is not widely accepted. This rather new sensation for me was unpleasant. For anyone who has experienced not fitting in, you'll understand what feeling I am referring to.

My mistake in my youth was to attempt to change who I was to stop this feeling. As I said in Chapter Two, people work to stop or suppress pain whenever and however they can. In looking back, it is easy for me to envision my twelve-year-old self thinking that by changing and thus fitting in, that I would be getting rid of this uncomfortable feeling.

What I didn't know at the time is that by changing how I acted, I didn't just not fit in with those around me, but I stopped fitting in with myself. This is when my feelings of loneliness became all too real, because up until that point, I had always honored my truths about who I am.

When I look back at the full picture of events, I can see through my own life experiences a new apple. While we can't control other people and their response to our unique selves, we can, through self-love, build a relationship with ourselves and always feel connected.

To achieve this connection there is a number of things that we can do. We can change the emotion we approach ourselves with, and thus how we perceive ourselves. We can work to re-write our inner dialogue, and more. This self-love we put into action transforms us into beings of love in a world of love.

Ultimately, we must see our truths and our wounds. I could not change paths years ago until I identified my rotten apple. We cannot break free of these rotten apples until we see them.

At the beginning of this book, I spoke of a different world, one where all we are is accepted and embraced. This approach to our light and darkness not only helps us to identify rotten apples, but it is what's required for us to achieve that authentic, healthy love we learned about in Chapter Four.

By accepting all we are, giving voice to what we once rejected within ourselves, we become more complete, we love more deeply, and we connect with a true love. A true love for ourselves.

What is Our Shadow?

We create danger for ourselves and others when we deny half of who we are. When we shy away from darkness, we limit and deny ourselves. Sometimes, in order to see and truly know the light, we must pass through darkness. If we are not afforded leeway to make mistakes, we shun life's gift.

Carl Gustav Jung, a Swiss psychiatrist who founded analytical psychology, introduced the idea of a shadow self.

> **SHADOW SELF:**
> Elements of our selves which have been rejected and feared, thus they have been pushed out of the light and into the darkness.

Through his work, Carl Jung discovered that in an effort to be loved and fit in, we have rejected parts of ourselves that our families, society, and even we ourselves view to be a hindrance to life, happiness, and love. As a result, we have split ourselves into the seen and unseen elements of our personality.

The Danger of the Shadow

However, as we've been discovering through the course of this book, when we deny an element of ourselves,
- We deny ourselves a healthy, authentic love.
- We have a hard time seeing our own worth.
- We allow our emotions, desires, and wounds to influence our life in subconscious ways. This keeps us from uncovering false wisdom, healing, and at times can endanger our happy lives.

Carl Jung believed we all carry a shadow self, but the depth and darkness is determined by the level and severity of how much of ourselves we shun. This shadow self consists of our secrets, shames, and repressed aspects. The parts deemed too evil, barbaric, shameful, sinful, or unacceptable to be honored or expressed.

CHAPTER 8: SELF-LOVE IN ACTION

Has there ever been a time when you've opened your mouth and something other than what you were thinking came out? Have you ever acted "out of character?" These are all instances when your shadow self has broken free and attempted to be heard and honored.

If you take a look at the Salem witch trials, you will see an instance where a culture supported the rejection of feminine power and sexuality (elements of the human experience) and suffered a collective shadow break because of it. Since these women accepted something others rejected, a collective feeling of fear and self-loathing pushed a group of people to lash out.

Carl Jung explains that when we reject a part of human life and see others openly accepting and embracing this element, we can snap and take our self-rejection and hate out on those people, as well as be driven to eradicate something that has been deemed harmful and dangerous.

Our Golden Shadow

While part of our shadow consists of the more primitive, self-centered, and violent aspects of human nature, Carl Jung believed that 90% of the shadow is "pure gold," or our Golden Shadow. That, in an effort to be accepted and loved, we have rejected elements of ourselves that might break the mold or display our unique selves.

We can end up repressing:
- Artistic talents.
- Sexuality and sensuality.
- Competitiveness.
- Innovative and free-thinking ideas.
- Intuition and even psychic abilities.
- Groundbreaking qualities.

All of which we reject when we believe they keep us from personal, familial, and social acceptance.

What is Shadow Work?

Shadow work is the process or practice of connecting with our inner darkness and working to embrace it and bring it back into the light. Through shadow work and authentic self-love, we develop a more holistic relationship with ourselves and heal the rifts within us. We embrace every facet of our being. In doing so, we transform our lives and so too our relationship with light and darkness. For our universe is still a place of duality. Yet this time…

Light is the love we have and the life we live in the external world.

Darkness is the aspects of ourselves yet to be discovered and the parts we keep for our inner circle. The deep parts of ourselves safe inside us, which we share with those we love and trust.

Over the course of this series, we will not only learn new wisdom, but through our self-love we will begin to shed light on and delve into our shadow. In doing so, we will not only reap the benefits of self-love, but will also change our culture to one of acceptance.

If you're interested in doing shadow work on your own, I strongly encourage you achieve a strong base of self-love first, because as you delve into the parts of you that have been hidden away, they will come with the knee-jerk reaction of rejection, hate, and even shame. It takes a strong sense of self-love, compassion, and forgiveness to reintroduce and combine these elements of yourself.

CHAPTER 8: SELF-LOVE IN ACTION

I would also recommend testing Carl Jung's work, because his personal philosophy is very much influenced by the life he lived. He perceived great darkness in people because he lived through World War II and witnessed the atrocities of that time.

The wonderful gift of self-love is not only that we can feel connected, accepted, and supported at all times, but that we can also choose how we go about loving ourselves. Which tools resonate with your personal style? Which pieces of wisdom will you utilize as new lenses through which to view your life?

What does it to mean to love yourself? What does it look like? How does it feel?

I asked these questions earlier in this book and my hope is that you have a better sense of what the answers are now. How will you love yourself? How might you alter these tools to better fit in with your personality? How does it feel to know that you are worthy?

Chapter Eight Takeaways: Self-Love in Action

- Vulnerability is not weakness but rather the most accurate measurement of a human being's courage.
- A life of love and expressing love is a vulnerable act.
- When we stop surviving, our emotions have room to be heard and honored.
- All emotions are a part of a healthy life. It is the manner in which we express these emotions that determines whether they are healthy or dysfunctional.
- We all have an inner voice that influences the condition of our life.
- We can use affirmations to heal and re-write our inner dialogue.
- Our perception of life influences our experience of life.
- Knowing yourself is one of the greatest acts of self-love, self-care, and a necessary building block to a thriving life.
- We can delve into who we are and our life through journaling.
- Self-advocacy is a necessary component to a healthy life.
- Boundaries are a form of self-advocacy.
- Shadow work is the process of shedding light on the hidden and rejected parts of ourselves. It not only is a great act of self-love but also helps display an authentic love.

CHAPTER 9

Healing and Life's Journey

write about what I know
that's why the stop and go

a part of me knows the truth
a part of me shakes in my boots

to continue on means to address
to take both feet and progress

which is silly to be sure
because both feet already
stand upon this path

to question the cause for my confusion
would be for me a lie

because what sends shivers and quakes
I can see most readily…

I fear I'm wrong and don't know
I fear the holes yet plugged,
will twist and turn the current

but most of all I fear it true
fear my past and what I might do

yet I know to face my fright is right
that my outcome and actions
won't be saved by loss of sight

so, I'm slowly twitching my toes
then more

till I brim full
and share my truth

slowly I will go

When we were young, we saw and understood life with a brightness and love. When asked what we were good at and who we were going to be when we grew up, we answered with the confidence of youth. Then there came the day when we traded in our youth and innocence for age and wisdom. No matter the age when this exchanged occurred, how we saw the world changed, and it has only continued to change.

The world, culture, and knowledge began to fill our minds, and in the process, we began to understand the logistics required to become that fireman or ballerina. To counteract this new knowledge, we created coping mechanisms for some of life's harsh truths and situations.

On this healing journey, I am asking you to change again. This time with conscious intention and purpose. So, rather than picking up rotten apples, you are picking up healthy wisdom, transforming you into a healthy person living a healthy life.

The First Question

In order to start this new transformation, there is the first question to consider.

>Are you ready to give up what ails you?

One of the hardest lessons I needed to learn was that not all people want to stop, turn around, face their dysfunction, and do something about it. That's why healers, shamans, and medicine women and men begin their sessions with this question.

Yes, a healer or doctor can recommend an herb or pill, can cut you open or realign a bone, or offer a new internal message. But they are not the ones who need to take the herb/pill, to stay in bed as the stitches heal, or to work to correct the inner dialogue going on inside.

At the end of the day, you are the only one around you 24 hours a day, 7 days a week, 365 days a year. At the end of the day, you are responsible and must decide if you're willing to give up what ails you.

Are you willing to give up:
- A thought?
- A habit?
- A harmful substance?
- A person?
- A place?
- The known to embrace the unknown?

The Role of a Healer

So, just what does a healer do, then? A healer offers aid, knowledge, and support. You do not need to walk this healing journey alone. You are not responsible for knowledge you have not yet been exposed to.

Just as a mechanic has specific knowledge to help you keep your car running smoothly, a healer seeks and learns knowledge, tools, and wisdom specific to their area of focus. So, when you need help, they can provide you with the:
- Knowledge
- Wisdom
- Aid
- Support
- Experience
- Third person perspective

that you need, so that you don't walk this path alone.

More specifically, a Medicine Woman like myself lives her life in connection with all of creation. (The community that we share.) As she lives her life, she offers her truth to the world, thus living by example.

As I was putting together my website, I was having a really hard time picking a name. This conundrum led me to sit down and define just what I was. I had studied to be a healer, and I was ready to share all this knowledge I had acquired on my own healing journey, but what was I, specifically?

When faced with this unknown answer, I went back to what I had done before: I sought out knowledge. What was the specific definition of shaman? Sage? Medicine woman?

When I came across an article on just what a medicine woman was, I knew I had found an accurate title for myself. As you know, I believe in the community that we share. I believe in living in harmony with all of life. I also love that while a medicine woman will share her truths with others, she doesn't use force. All of these elements already made up my understanding of life and how I lived it. I was and still am, by definition, a Medicine Woman.

Giving Up vs. Rejecting: A New Apple

In the first question we encounter the phrase, "give up" rather than "reject," and for those who have been raised in a harsher environment, it can seem too gentle of a way of expressing the act of letting go of old, rotten apples. So, take this moment with me to put these two apples to the test.

While the phrasing of the first question can alter from healer to healer, I prefer to ask, "Are you willing to give up what ails you?" I chose the wording to reflect not only the question but my personal philosophy.

By using the word "willing," I indicate the choice and personal power that we have to either step onto a healing path or avoid facing our dysfunction. I also chose the word "ails" because what we each need to release is dependent on what we have learned and the techniques we have used to cope.

For some, what ails them is a drug, for, others it's an idea, a person, or even a place. Often times, it can be a number of these things, or even a number of thoughts or people. Therefore, "ails" reflects whatever is currently in your basket of apples that is harming and impeding you and your chance at a thriving human experience.

Then we come to "give up." I chose this phrase over the word "reject" to indicate that we don't need anger, hatred, or harshness to change and heal. Rather than holding this rotten apple up to our eye and beating it up or yelling at it, we can we simply let go. By giving up this apple and letting it fall to the ground, we can continue on with our lives. In addition, we avoid a moment spent in anger, beating up an already bruised apple.

By choosing to give up what ails you, you simply release it; you walk on to new and brighter things. You ask your mind's eye to focus on the new and happy coming into your life, rather than pivoting to look at what you are leaving behind.

I would like to note that there are times when simply dropping the apple won't be enough. When it's superglued to your hand, more force will be required to let it go, to tackle the bigger ailments you are experiencing. If you encounter such a case, you can still approach things from a loving place.

Design your actions, words, and choices around your healing and not something's destruction. In this way, you are still able to stand up for yourself while looking forward to what's coming.

Our minds are powerful things, and they will look for what we seek. If we seek pain and problems, our mind will filter out all that doesn't qualify—like the good, happy, and safe people and things we have to be grateful for. By asking our minds to focus on the good, we naturally stop seeing and engaging with the ailments, making it that much easier to walk away.

In addition, sometimes an apple isn't rotten but simply not right for you. If you're homosexual, having an apple that says "heterosexual" harms you. It holds you to a standard that isn't healthy or accurate. But to reject this apple would cause harm to those who are heterosexual.

By choosing to merely give up this apple for a new and healthier one, you take care of you while also being a kind and supportive person. Some apples are rotten for us all and some are just a personal preference.

With all of that in mind, which apple do you choose? Will you set about your healing journey rejecting apples that don't work for you, or will you simply give them up and keep moving forward?

Giving Up the Known That No Longer Serves You

When we are children, we learn what works based on our limited experience of human life. We discover if…
- Temper tantrums get us what we want.
- Anger or sadness is more accepted.
- Gentleness or force is more respected.

The list goes on and on. But these perceived truths and coping mechanisms of our youth don't work as we grow into adulthood, if they ever worked at all.

Part of the healing journey is unlearning our:
- Coping mechanisms
- Habits
- Kneejerk reactions (emotional, mental, and physical.)

At the same time, we must learn new skills, tools, knowledge, perspectives, and work to create healthy habits out of them. To experience the benefits of this healing journey you need to be willing to release what you have known, what is comfortable to you even though it has been damaging.

By giving up the rotten apples you stop bringing pain into your life. You also create a space for new healthy, apples that will help you heal from the pain you encounter in life and the pain you sometimes brought into your life through human error.

While all of this information makes sense, I also know that if you are accustomed to rotten apples, the healthy ones can seem strange and foreign, leaving you yearning for a sense of the familiar, for that "at home" feeling.

But all we know, all that is familiar at one time started off as new and strange. Even speaking or walking took some time and practice.

My point is that, with a little time in unfamiliar territory, you have the opportunity to transform so that one day, you will not only be in familiar territory, but healthy territory, too.

Our Identity

While the crux of our healing is removing those rotten apples, when we release them, leaving them on the ground, we also release something else—our identities. Giving up what ails you includes giving up how you see yourself and the story you tell about yourself.

If you have lived with chronic pain, when you change your lifestyle and begin to heal, your understanding of yourself will change, as well. Sometimes we knowingly or even unknowingly utilize our pain as a crutch or a tool of manipulation.

I have personally known a couple people who have used their physical and mental ailments to manipulate situations to their benefit. They used statements like, "No I can't do X because of this ailment," or, "Would you please do X, you know I would, but I have this ailment," or, "My ailment is acting up again."

Some of these situations might be true; some of the emotional and physical pain might be real; but like the boy who cried wolf, people lose their credibility when they utilize their problems to their benefit and control. Especially when it is at the expense of others.

Releasing our ailments can be challenging and give us pause, since it means changing how we understand ourselves. While the thought of releasing your ailments might at first trigger fear, it also is an opportunity to be the type of person you imagine yourself to be, to be courageous, because trust me, releasing old rotten apples for new ones is courageous work.

Be willing to give up who you have known yourself to be in order to become a loving being. A person who is still you, but the version of you who lives a prosperous life.

Dare to Dream

The thing about communicating through a book is that I'm not sitting near you while I look you in the eye and tell you just how special you are. I don't know what you have lived through, suffered, or done. I don't know what silly thoughts or ideas are challenging these truths in your mind. I don't know how you're feeling, nor what your emotions are triggering in the way of thoughts and beliefs.

But I do know this: you're here, reading my second book. You have taken steps to challenge the old way of life for a new and healthier way of living. In the process, you have displayed the courage and strength to turn around and look at your life with open eyes and an open heart.

You are already transforming and becoming a being a love. On this healing journey we are traveling, I ask you to open your arms to new experiences and long-rejected elements of human life.

Transforming your life isn't just about doing the work, unlearning rotten apples, and acquiring new apples. It also means opening back up again and being vulnerable. One way we do that is by daring to dream.

When we were little kids, we treated ourselves in the manner we were shown. For most of us, this meant emulating loving and kind manners. We were comfortable sharing our strengths (anything we were interested in) and what we might do with our lives.

Through time, circumstances change, and unless we made a conscious point of hanging on to the childlike wonder, self-kindness, and excitement within us, we can lose touch with who we are and what brings us joy.

As you move forward with your life, open your arms wide to your inner child and let new and old dreams bubble up to the surface.

The Importance of Dreaming

While there are times to let go of dreams, such as discovering you don't have the ideal body type to be a ballerina, there are also times to pursue them. Choosing to pursue a dream not only provides us some direction, it also provides numerous benefits, even if the dream doesn't work or isn't completely fulfilled.

Some advantages to pursuing a dream include:
- You learn about what brings you joy and what interests you.
- You spend time immersed in meraki.
- You honor yourself.
- You demonstrate self-confidence and courage.
- You grow and strengthen within yourself.
- You inspire those around you.
- You might inspire an idea in someone else.
- You broaden the world.
- You just might discover where you belong.

Daring to dream means daring to be vulnerable and open. It means risking failure for the chance at another piece of a thriving life.

Enjoying the Journey

Life, living, connects us all the way to our souls. This human experience we are having is a journey. The eternity we have as souls also creates an overarching journey. Through these numerous journeys we develop this idea of an eternity and weave love within this idea, achieving a greater understanding of what existence means with a loving Spirit.

But as human beings we can often become complacent on our journey. We dance the steps robotically, rather than presently. By choosing to live in the present moment and enjoying whatever stage we find ourselves in, we experience the greatest benefits.

When I was young, I had purpose. I was a child and a student, and eventually an adult and a student—until the day came when I had no clear purpose. I became restless, unable to enjoy the moment, and I got too far out into the future. Due to all the unknowns and options I had available to me, I experienced panic and pain.

I ended up needing to learn how to break away from society's conventions and expectations and travel *my* journey. The one that is best for me.

As a result, I live my life experiencing balance between contentment with where I am on my healing journey and the journey of life. I also actively strive for more healing and happiness.

Balance

This balance can be strange to create, since it deviates from the norm, but when you find it, you discover a state of happiness. These days, I'm happy within the moments that make up my day. I'm happy hanging out with the people who have come to mean so much to me, and yet, I still gaze down my path to all that can be.

To my career and this book series. To having an avenue to pursue my purpose in this lifetime. To having stronger confidence and faith. To having wonderful friends and family. To learning new things. To choosing to be a being of love whose heart always remains in the present.

I can connect with all the people, activities, and things that are important and special to me when I choose to be present for each sensation the journey brings. I live a life that is designed to cherish the present while maintaining and building towards the future. I experience happiness today and make decisions that ensure that I continue to live a thriving life.

Balance: A New Apple

We often describe balance as the act of walking a tight rope. That one false move, one error in judgement or decision, will leave us plummeting down. Then the question becomes, do we have a net?

I dislike using this analogy. Sometimes we are out of balance. Sometimes, not every aspect of our life can be in balance. To then be condemned to falling off this rope doesn't demonstrate self-love or compassion.

We are here to learn and heal. To that end, we each have the right to human error. We will make mistakes, and even when we *don't* make mistakes, the manifestation of our balance will change to reflect where we are in our life's journey.

All of this has an impact on whether we are capable of finding that fine line that is balance. So, instead of walking a tightrope and hoping there is a net beneath us as we wobble and attempt to confine ourselves to this line, let us instead be dancers.

As dancers, we can ebb and flow to the song of life. To the quiet moments where we strike a pose and smile, to the boisterous moments where our feet may tap out noise in quick succession, from the mournful moments to the joyous ones.

Like any dancer, we will have moves we are already proficient in and ones that we're still learning. We will have moves we like and moves we don't, just as there are musical styles we appreciate and those we don't. Moments where our definition of balance will shift due to the music of life. The cycle of life.

When we are mourning the loss of a loved one, balance will mean more home time and less work time. When we are working towards a promotion, balance will mean more work time and less home time. Although it doesn't sound like it, this is balance.

- Single vs. with a partner.
- Employed vs. Unemployed.
- You, work, hobbies, family, friends, and obligations.

The fractions that portion out these various areas of your life generally aren't 50/50. Instead, they reflect our values and where we are on our life's journey. You may deem your self-care more important than work. However, all work, all you, all loved ones, all obligations, all hobbies is not balance. "Everything in moderation," right?

We are *practicing* balance. There's that word again. Practice. This means showing ourselves compassion and demonstrating self-love when we don't get it completely right.

With this new perception on balance, which apple will you choose for your basket? Will you be walking a tight-rope, or will you dance with the flow of life?

Honoring Cycles

The present is where we find life, where we experience and feel emotions. Living then becomes embracing the only thing that we have 100% for sure. Is that not why the "present" is a gift?

Woven within the present is structure not only for us to follow and utilize but also to provide depth to all of life. During the course of combining all I know, I have discovered that Spirit loves to cram as many blessings into one moment, situation, or experience as possible. This technique not only allows Spirit to utilize a single moment to its greatest potential, but it also weaves us together on a greater scale.

For Example,

Each time I go shopping for groceries, I finish my errands by waiting in line to check out. This simple moment is commonplace for most people. Yet, within this one moment there are many different elements.

Not only is there the top layer:
- Groceries.
- Work.
- Social interaction.
- External and Internal World.

But there's an undercurrent to the moment that addresses and honors our interwoven lives.
- We might hear or say something that shares the knowledge that we or another person needs.
- We might connect, proof that we are not alone.

- We might be presented with opportunities to learn and strengthen our love.
    - Chances to learn patience or self-advocacy.
    - Chances to display compassion or self-forgiveness.

Within a single moment we see evidence of life's complexity. We discover an undercurrent that addresses and honors the interwoven nature of life. Spirit does not just weave us together but utilizes the structure of cycles to continue to guide and support us.

When we attempt to separate ourselves from life's cycles, we separate ourselves from Spirit, health, happiness, and peace of mind. One way we can rediscover and enjoy our life's journey is to reconnect with this idea of cycles and utilize the structure found in cycles to help us navigate life.

Our life is in constant motion; we are constantly journeying through many cycles. When we learn to see these cycles for what they are, we are then able to discover how to ebb and flow, embracing the dance of life.

For Example
- **Cycle of a friendship:** A friendship that was great may be drawing to a close. When you are able to see this in your cycle, you can then honor the amazing time you had with this friend and still honor that it is time to part ways.

- **Cycle of a job:** As your friendship draws to a close, you may be starting a new job. One cycle is just beginning where the other is ending. How you act as you part and how you act as you begin will be significantly different. Here, you might choose to get to know your colleagues asking questions and spending time with one another.

- **Cycle of your relationship with your parents/children:** As you grow, your relationship with your parents changes to reflect where you are in your life. As time passes, you'll need less and less assistance in eating, getting around, and self-monitoring. When it is then your turn to become a parent, you will start caring for your child, and as the years pass, provide them opportunities to learn self-reliance and resiliency, thus returning the gifts your parents gave you.

When we get stuck in a cycle that has passed or refuse to continue on, we do ourselves, others, and our relationships a disservice. As children become more independent, using their parents as a crutch has the potential to ruin the relationship and doesn't set themselves up for a healthy life. The same is true for parents who don't relinquish control to their children as they grow up. Both are a recipe for hardship, which can be avoided by not only loving our family members but demonstrating this love in a healthy way, by honoring where everyone is in their individual cycles.

Just as our relationships follow cycles and changes as we grow and age, we also experience a set of cycles in connection with Mother Earth.

- **Cycle in the year:** The seasons shift, but we have stopped transitioning with them. Instead of honoring the hibernation aspects of winter, we go, go, go, then continue to go, go, go into the summer. As beings of Earth, our bodies have a cycle that is closely tied to where the Earth is in *her* cycle. Our bodies, minds, emotions, and our souls need time to rest. I'm not saying don't do anything in winter; rather, honor the season, honor your balance, and honor yourself and what you need. This is self-love in action.

- **Cycle in the month:** The energy of the moon impacts the tides, so it most definitely has the ability to impact us. The moon's energetic impact changes over the course of its cycle. As a direct result, our energy changes over the course of a month. When we choose to take the time to reconnect with the cycle of the moon, we can achieve a greater understanding of how we are feeling and what we're going through.

- **Cycle in the week:** While manmade, weeks create a structure where most of us spend weekends relaxing and weekdays at work. Our week has a cycle of a start, middle and end, with an amalgamation of work and relaxation. By aligning your plans with the cycle of a week, you can honor your work while also honoring rest and recuperation.

The Purpose of Cycles

As you can see, there is a flow and rhythm to the various elements in our lives, from our relationships to the Earth's revolution in the Universe. Not only do these structures create guidance for us, but they also create guidance for Spirit and our spirit guides.

By knowing and respecting the cycle of things, we work in tandem with life, not only receiving guidance as we navigate life, but also cultivating harmony. Spirit and our spirit guides can use this same structure to anticipate where we are in our individual cycles and where we are going in our lives.

Spirit guides can then make choices and provide guidance with greater clarity. They not only know where we're headed due to the cycle we're in, but also due to our soul contract. From this insight they are able to pass on information, guide us, prepare our way, and call in other spirit guides for a hand.

Cycles are everywhere and can be found even in the process of grocery shopping. They not only aid us as we navigate life but provide growth and depth to our lives.

The Uncompleted Cycle

While living your life in alignment with cycles is important, not all cycles are completed—especially when these cycles become toxic, dysfunctional, or even irrelevant to who you have become and where you are going with your life.

Just because you have invested time and energy (and maybe even money) doesn't mean that completing the cycle is what's best for you. For example, there is a healer in my local community who has been married three times. Now, in the society I live in, this number of divorces and remarriages is synonymous with "failure." But according to this healer, they were relationships with past karma and each marriage took care of the karma. Once these lessons were taught and learned, it didn't serve her well to stay married.

Whether it's a marriage that is no longer healthy or relevant, a relationship, or a job, sometimes what's best is to walk away. Leaving a cycle uncompleted is not always a sign of "failure," but rather a sign of healing, strength, and love. Yes, you love that other person or your job, but you love yourself more.

The In-Between

Woven within the cycles we travel are moments of in-between. As we spiral through our cycles in a circular motion, each pass has the potential to bring us to a higher level. Within each pass we not only grow but can enter into a period of transition.

While the in-between is a natural part of life, it can also be an ignored and neglected element of life--especially when we aren't honoring ourselves. The same can be said of the reverse, where we can end up spending too much time in-between our cycles. As a natural part of life, there is value to be found when we honor the moments that are in-between.

What is the "In-Between"?

An in-between moment can be as large or small as is necessary. It encompasses the time where we are in the process of transition or recovery. Since there is no set time limit, if we don't connect with where we are in life and embrace this truth, we can end up comparing our experiences to that of others.

When we utilize other's experiences in a healthy manner, they can act as a method of guidance. If you're going through your first break-up, a shift in careers, or if your kids have moved out of the house, these changes represent new situations. In these instances, you can utilize other's experiences to provide you with an idea of what to expect.

But if we attempt to align our timeframe with another's experience or even with what we desire, we are left in disharmony. Each stage in our life takes the time it is meant to, as long as we don't fight the natural flow of creation.

Example One

A common example of not choosing to honor our in-between and our own pace comes when we experience grief. The time it takes to process and let go of our sorrow is individual and personal. Choosing to rush this time, because of other's expectations or our own, stunts our growth, healing, and overall wellness.

We can also rush the in-between when we lack faith and conviction, when we choose not to trust the path and choices we have made. We can even go so far as to skip an in-between period altogether, or choose to run back to what we have left, just because the fear of taking that leap of faith, or the idea of being without or alone, terrifies us.

Example Two

When we encounter the end of a relationship's cycle, especially a romantic relationship, we can choose to either remain in the relationship or promptly return to that individual we are no longer happy with, due to our fear of being alone or of the unknown. Or we can do the opposite and jump from one relationship straight into another to avoid that "alone" time.

In either case, we don't experience any grieving time. If we went back to what we had, we stall our cycle and delay moving on. This approach doesn't fix our problem and puts us in a dangerous place.

If we did jump right into new arms, we wouldn't spend any time reflecting on what didn't work last time. We would fail to give ourselves the opportunity to update our techniques, needs, desires, and expectations. We also don't spend any time recuperating and healing from any pain we may have sustained—or caused.

Oftentimes, we jump into a relationship with the same person or job as last time, just a different version. Since we didn't spend time re-evaluating what we want from our relationship or job, we follow the same steps and selection process we used last time. When we do that, we get the same results, which means we know how it will work out.

When we choose to honor our in-between time, preparing beforehand (creating a financial nest egg, collecting all your things) and using the time as intended (grieving, healing, learning, and growing) we come to the start of our next cycle grown, healed or healing, and happy. In these instances, we not only honor and complete a cycle, but we also reach the next level, thus traveling upwards like a spiral.

This increases the chances that our next cycle will be healthier and happier. It also increases the odds that we learned the lesson intended during the previous experience and so we need not repeat the lesson.

The in-betweens last for a moment, but it's important to remember that they end. Forever having an in-between is not healthy. An in-between can last years, but if you refuse to take the next step when the time is right, you miss an avenue in your life to engage with life.

How are you at honoring your in-between time?

What to Do In An In-Between Period As A Being Of Love

When we choose to live as beings of love, we can oftentimes feel the need to give love. We temper this by regulating how much love we show someone based on who they are and our personal connection to them. But when we find ourselves at a crossroads, where who and what we know is in flux, we enter into an in-between period.

Due to the nature of an in-between period, we can experience a time where no one feels close to us and as such, we feel that there is no one in our lives to love. As beings of love, we can feel as if we might drown or overflow with the love that we have to give, so we can end up giving our love to memories. This creates a myriad of problems even as it solves our drowning sensation. For when we deposit much of our love and heart to the moments, events, and people of the past, we:

- May return to those in the past, despite them no-longer being healthy or positive for us.
- Become emotionally unavailable and then never truly reach a place where we have new people to connect with. The ones who would meet us loving dose for loving dose can see that while we have love to give, we are not in a place to meet them at their level of commitment and strength, because most of our love is tied up with the past. Due to these circumstances, we won't attract new people who can and will love us with the same ferocity.
- Or, we end up settling on those who *can* meet our love for love ratio when part of our love is invested on memories, which can cause imbalance in the relationship. Ultimately, this can create an unsavory recipe that leaves us in a relationship with someone not at our level of love, or has us ending another relationship on the heels of our old one.

We lose sight of the truth about the people from our past, we endanger ourselves, and we get into such a muddled state about the present. We must stop, and we also must not drown. So, what do we do?

We invest our love as we have before, but we invest in people who are part of our present. While we're in this in-between period, we must take all the love that we are capable of and:
- Invest in those still here.
- Invest more on healthy acquaintances who just might be friend- worthy.
- Take the bulk of your love that's left and invest it in yourself.

Turn the tables and rather than drowning, love with all that your heart has to offer. Love yourself; step up your game.

Invest In Yourself:
- Display compassion for wounds you've sustained.
- Forgive and accept the mistakes you've made, including how long it took you to walk away and make a change.
- Invest energy and interest in the lessons and growth available.
- Show support for things you've learned about life, yourself, and others.
- Pursue your passions and interests (meraki).
- Try a new hobby or travel to a desired destination or experience.

The length of an in-between period will be determined by three things:

One: The time it takes to grieve, learn, let go, heal, and prepare (to a degree) for those new opportunities for love on the horizon.

Two: Your stubbornness and fear, how long it takes you will be influenced by how invested and open you are to the transformation that is occurring.

Three: Spirit's timing. Our soul contract and the influence of the external world (the bigger picture) influences the timing of this in-between period, which means that it can be longer or shorter than we anticipate or desire.

The healing, readiness, and growth you enjoy from embracing the in-between period is directly related to how you choose to experience the moment. You have the free will to live in the moment or to fight against it. Remember how my mom likes to say, "it's not the event but how you perceive it." This chosen perception determines the quality and nature of our experience.

Then, as you exit this in-between period, you will enter into a new cycle and have an opportunity to redistribute your love once more. You'll be in the position to continue honoring your heart and give love:

- To those who are still by your side, who stuck by and supported you before and during your in-between moment.
- To those you met during your in-between period. Perhaps now you're open to investing more than common courtesy-and-acquaintance-level love (one spoonful; xenia).
- To yourself—always keep loving yourself.
- To the new people or things that have entered this new cycle in your journey.

What you'll discover is that as you healed and grew during this in-between period, you haven't just transformed due to the changes you made, but also due to what you experienced during that time. You come out as a different person on the other side.

You have…
- Grown.
- Become wiser.
- Released some dysfunction.
- Replaced some dysfunction with healing and healthy techniques.

You will discover that through this experience, your heart and your love has grown, too. Your love of self has grown and become more consistent. You've healed new and old wounds, and now your heart is more resilient.

This exercise of love (active love) has strengthened and stretched your heart and you now have more to offer. By acting in love, you've been shaping your environment and reality and helping the world, too, thus honoring every aspect of the human experience.

Celebration

Life is what we make of it. How we shape our thoughts and actions molds the world around us. Imagine for a moment a mound of clay that lays upon its spinning stand. Our thoughts—the picture we hold in our minds—is going to influence and define the actions we take to bring this idea in our head to life.

This vision may change shape, but it creates the framework of what we are creating. Our thoughts, whether they are of a poor-lifeless creation or of a vibrant-joyous creation, will determine what we build, as our thoughts propel energy outwards, and we manifest what we see.

By taking our hands and sliding them against the clay, applying pressure with our fingertips and our palms, we bring the clay mound into a round stub. Clay coats our hands and as the table turns our mound of clay around and around, our actions build what we envision.

Shifting our hands, we place a single thumb into the center of our mound and then the other. Slowly, we draw our hands deeper and farther up. A base now connects the clay to our plate. Further upwards we draw our hands, pulling our thumbs apart, stretching the opening.

Around and around our clay rotates until the mound of clay no-longer exists. From the image that we pictured and the actions we have taken, a chalice sits on the plate. Deep and tall, the stalk fills our grip, the basin stretches outwards and holds within it the great potential for all things.

Taking wire, we slice the stalk of our chalice away from the plate, allow it to dry, and then place it within the kiln. Baking dry, our creation manifests itself until what exists in the grip of our hand is potential.

Our chalice has the opportunity to overflow with love and joy. To inspire us to lift our arms and celebrate every aspect of life. To clink with our friends and family in celebration. Our creation, our every breath, and our life has the potential to overflow. Life can be an act of celebration.

Examples of Small Celebrations
- I know a family that has a summer temperature rule. When the temperature reaches above 75 degrees Fahrenheit, they sometimes celebrate by going out for ice cream.
- When we get a new haircut, clothes, or item of importance to us, we can do a happy dance.
- Due to the fact that my family doesn't drink alcohol, we choose to instead drink organic sparkling apple cider to celebrate.

Whether you are celebrating something big filled with traditions or something small, you can influence how many hours a week you spend practicing happiness. By taking the time to celebrate, you not only get all of those good vibes to enjoy, but you also create a culture in your village that puts an emphasis on joy rather than fear.

You connect deeply with those you love when you celebrate. By incorporating their traditions into your celebration or just by taking the time to be a part of their lives, you weave them into your life and heart.

The Healing Journey

Once we acknowledge that we aren't where we wish to be in our lives and decide to face our dysfunction and give up what ails us, we begin a cycle known as a healing journey. While each healing journey that we travel in our lives is unique to who we are, where we are in our lives, and the ailment we are healing, all healing journeys share similar elements, creating not only a cycle but a structure.

This structure consists of:
- **Identification:** We identify that something is wrong, wounded, or not in alignment with our dream.

- **Decision:** We decide to turn and face our hurt and heal, giving up what ails us.

- **Healing:** The tools and knowledge we utilize to heal is an amalgamation of what we know, what we have used before, and what we will learn now. Since each wound (physical, mental, emotional, spiritual) is unique, the best method for healing will reflect what wound we are addressing.

- **Backsliding:** Like a physical wound that we can scratch at or a torn ligament that we overextend too soon, we can sometimes fall back into patterns that are no longer good for us. While this might trigger shame, guilt, or a sense of failure, when we view the situation through the eyes of love, we learn compassion, and we can see that backsliding is a natural part of any cycle.

- **Health and Transformation:** Once we've addressed our wounds, we heal. The level of healing and how we have healed will also trigger change. When we release what doesn't work for us, we often times learn new things to replace this new gap in knowledge. In the process, we heal, change, and transform.

Right now, you and I are on a healing journey to address the root cause of most of our ailments. In the process, we are transforming into beings of love, living a Heart-Centered Life. By achieving this personalized thriving human experience, we not only create a wonderful life for ourselves, but put into place plans and techniques to perpetuate this wonder.

As you travel on your healing journey, embrace where you are right now and know that the work and dedication you put in is taking you through a cycle that will lead you to a better world, self, and life.

Time and The Healing Journey

While it only took five bullet points to identify the various steps to a healing cycle, the reality of any healing journey it much more complex. Whether it is a small healing cycle to address a rug burn or stubbed toe, or a larger cycle like a broken heart, it takes time to heal. It takes a lot of time to heal our very understanding of human life.

Since we know that healing takes time, give the gift of time to yourself. In doing so you practice self-care while choosing to work in tandem with the nature of reality.

> In time the glaciers shaped our mountains and rivers.
> In time animals have evolved.
> In time humankind has come to be.
> In time diamonds are formed.
> In time wounds heal and scars fade.
> In time we learn and grow.

Things take time, so as you walk this healing journey, give yourself time to heal. You won't have all the answers tomorrow, but if you never look, you'll never find the answers at all. It is through time and work that we can be like the rivers and carve ourselves a wonderful life.

Divine Timing

Over the last few years, I've come to learn an important component to time. I have discovered that time is on Spirit's side. As I have traveled my personal career cycle, there have been many moments where I have wanted things to move faster or slower, to have more information, or to see the moving pieces.

When I started, I just wanted answers about what to do with my life. I didn't envision a book—that came later—nor did I envision the steps I would take or that I would move during the process.

If it had been left up to me, learning I would write a book, writing it, and publishing it would have happened much faster. But of course, my timeline did not match Spirit's, and Spirit was right.

Looking back, knowing what I know now, I realize that it would not have been healthy or smart to impart the information I desired when I wanted it. Nor would it have been smart to publish when I thought I would. In this instance I was blind, lost in the darkness, and ultimately it was for the best.

Instead, I didn't publish with a publishing house. I'm an indie self-publisher. I didn't publish a book but created a series, and I didn't publish my first book until it was the right time.

Here's the thing: we don't see all the moving pieces and as human beings we aren't able to know everything. Sometimes, we don't even know what's best for us, which is why we need to develop a relationship with someone who does. By changing our perception about our life and developing a relationship with Spirit, we can live happily.

When I first started my career cycle, I wanted information, and I made decisions based on what I knew. Through time, I learned more, and my decisions and what I have ended up creating have transformed into something beyond my imagination. Just like we ask for the "most benevolent outcome for all involved" because we don't hold all the answers, we too need to trust in divine timing, because Spirit has our back always. This way we can relax, be free of fear, and live a thriving human experience.

CHAPTER 9: HEALING AND LIFE'S JOURNEY

The Boarding Pass Analogy

Whenever my fear and old rotten apples attempt to overtake me, my mom helps remind me about divine timing by utilizing the boarding pass analogy. She helps me to remember that just because it doesn't make sense to me, there is a plan and structure guiding and supporting me.

Imagine that you are taking a trip with your family. After a family meeting, you have been tasked to take care of the children in your family. Since you're in charge, it is your responsibility to make sure the kids make it onto the plane.

Since these kids are older, they want the responsibility of showing their boarding pass to the flight attendant as they get on the plane. So, when do you give them their plane ticket?

- When you reach the airport before checking your bag?
- When you reach security?
- When you reach your gate and proceed to wait for another hour?
- Or right when you board the plane?

Just as you have the responsibility to look out for these kids, who feel grown up but still might drop or misplace their boarding pass, Spirit has the responsibility to guide and protect us. This sometimes means withholding vital pieces of information or materials until the right moment. In this case, the right moment is when it's time for us to board the plane.

Had Spirit told me four years ago that I would be an Energy Healer and author, my 19-year-old self would have had a massive panic attack. Four years ago, I wasn't ready; it wasn't the right time. Spirit knew this even as I didn't. It wasn't until the right time for me that I was brought into the loop of what I had agreed to do in this lifetime when I created my soul contract.

Your timeline and Spirit's may not match, but I have yet to see or experience Spirit's timeline as wrong. So, when you struggle with the timing of things, ask yourself, do you want your timeline or Spirit's informed timeline? Is it time for you to be handed that boarding pass?

Backsliding

When we took a look at the cycle of a healing journey, we discovered backsliding. Unfortunately, many of us possess a very rotten perception on what backsliding means.

The Rotten Apple: Backsliding Means:
- Failure.
- Shame.
- Guilt.

In addition to these inaccurate and toxic emotions, we have created false ideas due to the toxic environment surrounding backsliding.

Thoughts that:
- We must get "it" (lesson, skill, ability) on the first try.
- That once we get "it" we don't ever need to re-learn or study it.

Not only does this create a toxic truth for us in life, but we see evidence of this rotten apple in our education system. If you take a moment to think back to school, you might discover that the curriculum focused on a subject (like adverbs) and gave you a work sheet and maybe a packet, but didn't teach you how to identify and use adverbs again. Yet, this information was on the test.

With a single "truth" (rotten apple), we have created an environment that challenges us rather than supports us. So instead, let's test our understanding of backsliding.

What is Backsliding?

As you can see, while backsliding is a part of any learning cycle, our perception of the word and idea can be rotten. Sometimes a rotten apple is not an idea but rather our understanding of it.

So… what is backsliding?

When we look through the eyes of love, we discover that backsliding is not a bad thing, but rather a natural component to growth. If we were to choose the rotten idea of backsliding, we would just be inviting unnecessary drama and pain into our lives. But don't just take my word for it. Instead, put my understanding of backsliding to the test.

Conclusion

Backsliding is a natural part of the process in any learning cycle.

Argument

Despite the negative connotation backsliding has received, we've been backsliding all our lives. We've been ebbing and flowing between:
- Infant and child.
- Child and teenager.
- Teenager and adult.
- Adult and elder.

Since we first attempted to speak and walk, we have experienced backsliding. Through the years, as we have continued to grow, we have only backslid more.

There were days when we felt big and grown, ready to step out into the world and face whatever adventures awaited. Then, just as easily, we awoke feeling small and insecure, choosing to hide behind our parent's pant leg or ask for help with our work. What moments can you think of from your own life?

Then, consider this…if backsliding has been a part of our lives since the very beginning, and Spirit is loving, then would Spirit incorporate something like backsliding in our lives if it was bad?

If we were to transform our understanding of backsliding and thus change our perception, we might identify backsliding as a part of any cycle. So, when we do experience this element in our lives, through compassion and self-love, we can give ourselves and others a break to honor the truth of human error and backsliding.

Why We Backslide

It is easy to fall back into old thought patterns and habits that are no longer good for us. We also can backslide when we're still learning a new tool, skill, or fulfilling obligations in conjunction with being an adult.

All of these different scenarios carry with them an opportunity to practice self-love and compassion. To choose how you will perceive the moment and thus how you will experience it.

Plus, a lot of our life is habitual. Do you look at a map every time you drive, or is it a habit to take this turn, then that one? Do you look at a recipe every time you cook your favorite dish?

I actually just did this a few years ago. I was making an old cake mix I used to use and pulled out all of the ingredients I needed.

But it wasn't until I checked the box that I found that they had changed the mix. What was once a softened stick of butter had become a ⅓ cup of melted butter.

Thankfully, the mix came out alright, and later on I would learn how to make a cake from scratch, but that moment could have been a moment of failure. Instead, I chose to display compassion for myself, and can look back on that memory as proof positive that mistakes and backsliding in skills—like baking a cake—is a natural part of life.

Reasons We Backslide

One: The old way of doing things is familiar.

The new way of thinking or acting requires time before it feels familiar. Sometimes, after a hard day, we want that old, comforting way of doing things, even if we know that way to be a thing of our past that is no longer good for us.

Two: The people around us impact our journey just as we impact theirs.

When you decide to change things, the people around you are going to experience changes in their life. They can either accept or reject these changes, but in either case, those around us are now in a situation where transitions are occurring.

If you start re-writing the rules on how other people are to interact with you, they will need some time to get used to it. Or, they just won't like it. If you start setting up boundaries, saying "no," ending old toxic relationships, and expecting more for yourself and from others, you are going to send out ripples impacting people around you.

They may attempt to stop these changes; they might lash out. Sometimes, we'll miss the people we've chosen to let go of because they are no-longer good for us, or never were.

In any variation of this situation, we can experience backsliding. If we were to choose a fear-based perception, we would then be condemned to shame and failure, but if we look from a place of love, we can redirect our behavior and keep growing all without needing to experience a moment of shame.

Three: We can doubt and question our self-worth and right to dream.

We all have a right to be happy and healthy. But we can backslide and go back to things that are not good for us when we doubt that we have a right to move on. Self-sabotage is deadly and very, very sneaky.

In that event, when backsliding happens, we need to remember that we are "practicing." Our growth and change lead us to a different life, but as we journey to that new state of being and self-worth, we are learning how to be healthy.

Four: We can be tired and our personal best might be less than it was yesterday.

When we lack the energy to make conscious decisions to create the changes we desire, we can end up going back to the old ways of doing things or to the person we have left. In either case, when we wake in the morning rested and with energy, we can choose to spend our morning berating ourselves for being human, or we can choose actions and words that will place us back on the path of healing.

Five: We remember the past after the pain has passed and recall the happy moments.

Possibly one of the most complicated ways we backslide is when the memories are great. When we have outgrown old relationships/jobs or when our paths diverge, it can be hard to let go and move on. Often times, dysfunctional or even outdated relationships weren't all bad. They brought with them happy experiences, which make for happy memories.

For example, I had a best friend all through middle and high school. We were friends for almost eight years until our lives diverged onto two separate paths that have taken us in two different directions. There was no big fight or disagreement, we merely drifted and couldn't seem to find a way to stay connected.

We created many wonderful memories, so letting go was truly difficult, especially when I then entered an in-between period. In this instance, I understand how the pull of what was can be strong enough to bring us to call and see those with whom we are no longer close. If you experience a moment like this, remind yourself why you're on this healing journey.

We can end up backsliding for so many different reasons in many different scenarios. So, when you backslide, put the energy into returning to what's good and healthy for you now. Be gentle and kind to yourself. It's only an "end of the world" moment if you treat it as such.

By choosing to approach my life from this new perspective, I am demonstrating self-love. I am not forcing myself to be perfect, I am not holding myself to a standard I cannot achieve, and I am not shaming or guilt tripping myself for being where I am. Instead, I choose to trust in myself and my diving timing.

Whether we are backsliding, experiencing an in-between period, or completing or entering into a new cycle, when we choose to honor where we are in life, we open the door to happiness. We begin to live in the present moment, and while we walk this journey of healing, we experience joy.

Chapter Nine Takeaways: Healing and Life's Journey

- Before we help others or go about healing ourselves, it is important that we ask, "Are you ready to give up what ails you?"
- Since we are each responsible for our own lives and healing, the role of any healer is to provide knowledge, guidance, and support as we take our healing journeys.
- As we heal, we transform, and it becomes necessary to give up what we know in order to embrace a healthier reality. Sometimes this includes our very identity.
- As we heal, we open ourselves up to a whole new set of possibilities. In order to live a life based upon your desires, you need to dream.
- Life is a constant journey, and we have the choice to either fight against it or enjoy it.
- A New Apple: Balance can be a dance rather than walking on a tightrope.
- Life is filled with cycles which provide structure and guidance, not only for us but for our support team (Spirit and spirit guides).

- At the end of a cycle, we encounter an in-between period. When we honor that period, we heal, learn, grow, and reduce the likelihood that we'll repeat the same mistakes.
- Every healing journey takes time, but we can choose to enjoy where we are in the cycle. Not only does this improve the quality of our lives, but it honors divine timing.
- Divine timing is the timing we experience based on Spirit and the expansive knowledge Spirit possesses.
- Backsliding is a natural part of human life and rather than perceiving it as a sign of failure, we can choose the path of love and compassion.

CHAPTER 10

Manifestation – How it All Looks

my body calls out
my soul attempts to reach me
within myself I reach out–
the neglect lies bare

in this moment
I kneel upon a crossroads
do I turn away
or do I dare look

fill my sight
with my past
and present state

if I look
can I discover the love
I carry within

touch it
let it shine upon my face
and allow it to work
its healing magic

allow it to transform
my very reality

that upon this new path
with new eyes and heart
the mist of fear may depart

and what I am left to see
is indeed a wonderful world

Throughout history we have crafted and lived our lives based on diverse cultures. Small villages developed a culture centered around the individual and how their lives wove within the village. These varied cultures honored two fundamental truths: that we are part of a community, and that the quality of human life increases when this truth is honored.

In these villages, the chief provided physical nourishment and safety while the medicine woman worked hard to provide for her people in another way. Together, the village wove a nurturing environment meant to cultivate a wonderful life for each individual.

Through time and transforming cultures, the role of Medicine Woman or any healer has shifted. With new techniques, tools, knowledge, and technology available, the manner in which healers operate has changed dramatically. As a result, we each have the resources at our disposal to build a unique method to healing.

Yet what has remained the same through the ages and amidst varying cultures and climates is that we are storytellers. Through the stories we share, hear, and witness, we learn and grow. Whether we tell them in the form of a picture, song, dance, book, or through oral tradition, we convey knowledge about the human experience.

As a medicine woman, I not only share the knowledge I have collected over the years, but my story, as well. My story has become wonderous because I choose to dream, to seek out the tools and knowledge that will bring me healing and joy.

Just like me, you too have a story, one that is designed to help you pursue your own dreams by embarking on a healing journey. While it may not be a dream of glass slippers, a prince, or a fairy godmother, it still is a story worth telling, because it is the story of your life.

Together, we can share our stories and the stories that have touched us. In this way, we will not only experience a healing journey, but will encounter the tools and knowledge we need to reach our dreams along the way.

What's Your Story?

We tell ourselves all kinds of stories, from how the world works to who we are. The thing about stories is that when we read them or see them on the movie screen, they can be about anything and anyone. Yet, when we tell ourselves the story of life, the human experience, and our lives, the story's content matters.

If our story falls into the category of fiction, we're in trouble. Who we are, our character, personality, and identity, transforms during the course of our lives, and it is important that we stay up to date with the story we tell ourselves.

Alert: Rotten Apples

Utilizing a story about ourselves that is riddled with fiction puts us in a dangerous place. Not only does our perception and understanding of life and ourselves become skewed, but we can create problems and pain on account of this.

One: Denying the Truth of Change

If we tell ourselves that our life and who we are will never change, we then deny the simple truth of change. Change is possible and with time, probable. By denying this truth, we create a rotten apple for ourselves that either condemns us to a surviving human life (since we won't ever change) or blinds us to the dedication we need to maintain and cultivate a growing and thriving prosperity.

The story you tell yourself today will change in order to remain accurate, just as the story you told ten years ago reflected a different version of you and your life. Give yourself the right to change the story you tell, to not only honor the truth of change, but to also empower yourself.

Two: We End Up with Masks

If the story we tell ourselves about our life and the lives of those around us is based on lies or half-truths, we not only miss out on authentic love, but we create a divide rather than connection. Through these half-truths and lies, we become blind to not only the true nature of things, but to who we and others truly are.

Due to misidentification or blindness, we lack the necessary knowledge we need to identify our wounds and problems. We are then unable to make the changes we need to create and maintain a thriving life. If we can't see the problem or wound, we can't address it and heal.

Three: We Become Lost

When the story we tell of ourselves is fictitious, we become lost to the truth of who we are. As we've seen, self-knowledge and acceptance are necessary for self-love and a life of prosperity.

By utilizing a false story, we become divided from the knowledge of who we are and what brings us joy. As a result, we can feel lost in life, not sure where we fit in or what to do with ourselves. This limiting life story not only doesn't serve us well but can also limit the potential we have in life, for our dreams will also be lost.

Four: We Create Absolutes

As we tell our story we can create absolutes out of unknowns. What I mean by this is that as human beings, we don't know everything. Due to this fact, some of the elements in our life cannot be known completely, but in an attempt to control and define our lives, we create absolute statements about them.

For example, if you've suffered trauma and then tell your story as being "wounded, disfigured, or broken," you live your life based on these "truths." You've taken an unknown element in your life and rather than giving yourself an opportunity to heal, you've created an absolute: that you are wounded.

Just as the definitive statement of being broken rather than having been wounded keeps pain in the moment, definitive statements about healing can be just as debilitating. When we tell the story of us "getting all better," we create an absolute out of something that cannot be known. Sometimes, our story needs to leave some answers open to the unknown.

For Example

In the 6th grade, I had an allergic reaction to a tetanus booster shot and chicken pox vaccine and suffered a seizure. Not only was the experience traumatizing, but it was accompanied with a horrible nightmare that I had during the seizure. As a result of this trauma, I developed a massive phobia of needles.

At that time, I couldn't talk about, see pictures, or movie clips about needles without hyperventilating. My fear was limited to medical needles; I was cool with sewing needles. Phobias are quirky that way.

Had I chosen to live my life with this "truth," I would be panicking as I wrote these words, but I left my story about my phobia open to the unknown and through time and exposure, I consistently have gotten better.

Through time, my phobia made itself known when I thought about needles, but as I healed, I reached a place where I could talk about them. Through continued exposure I cried through my blood draw but later only fainted for my second ear piercing. While each experience was hard, I approached each moment as an opportunity to heal and stayed open to the unknown.

Today, I don't hyperventilate about needles; I don't cry or faint anymore. I still need to practice a deep style of meditation and must prepare myself in advance, but I didn't write my story as being stuck with a phobia. Instead, I left myself open to the unknown, thus giving myself permission to travel past a story of pain and onto a fairytale.

How to Tell Your Story

As you can see, our perception and how we tell the story of our lives matters. Our retelling impacts how we perceive our lives and thus, how we experience them. So, I have a few pointers on how you can approach your story...

The Past
- Tell it as it was.
- This means including the good and bad, working to avoid half-truths and lies. This clarity will also aid you in healing and authentic self-love.
- Perceive and approach your past from a place of love by choosing to display compassion and forgiveness for yourself and others.

The Present
- Tell it as it is.
- Give voice to what you are working on and the dreams you have.
- Spread your arms and heart wide open to life.

- Open up your story to the unknown of the future and allow Spirit and your spirit guides space to work their miracles.

The Future
- Talk about where you dream of going.
- Provide enough structure to help guide you moving forward, while leaving room for the unknown.

What is your story?

Breaking Down the Path of Happiness: The Big Picture

We are forever growing and building on our life's journey. Within a single lifetime we have many cycles and smaller journeys, like our current healing journey, that weave together to form a full and personalized life.

Through this healing journey we wish to achieve the destination or end result of a thriving human experience. But whenever we reach a destination, it merely acts as a pit-stop on our journey.

If we limit our happiness to a destination, we spend the majority of our lives (the journey) in a different kind of human experience. Since we desire a life filled to the brim with happiness, instead of limiting ourselves to destinations, let's choose a Path of Happiness.

In doing, so we achieve:
- Living in the moment, where life is happening.
- Living in a manner that we desire; one of happiness, love, and healing.

- The ability to honor the needs of the future to come: budgeting so we have money, putting plans in place to manifest our dreams, learning new tools and skills, etc.
- Enjoying the human experience that we're building today and all the days to come.

> **YOUR PATH OF HAPPINESS:**
> The journey or path you travel that celebrates the human experience you are living, while also building towards greater moments to come, ensuring you continue to live that wonderful thriving human experience.

In choosing to walk the Path of Happiness, you are choosing to create a world that supports and loves you today and all the days to come. In this way, you weave happiness, love, and healing into your very journey, rather than treating these elements of human life as destinations.

Yes, there will still be sad days and hard life experiences, but with a personalized Path of Happiness, you not only have a strong personal philosophy guiding you, but you have an environment internally and externally designed to help get you through the hard stuff and celebrate all the good. In essence, this is the big picture structure that you can choose to guide you and help you cultivate the good things in life.

The Three Keys to a Strong and Successful Path of Happiness

Through my own personal healing journey, I have discovered that there are Three Key components to building a strong structure for our human experience. While our personal philosophy will provide us the knowledge and tools we need to understand and navigate the world, these Three Keys remain constant even as our lives change.

The Three Keys:
- Know Yourself.
- Love Yourself.
- Spiritual Connection.

Know Yourself

As we've seen through self-love, when we take the time and apply dedication to our relationship with ourselves, we reap numerous benefits. By knowing who you are, who you desire to be, and how you perceive the world, this information and insight guides you to a personal life of happiness.

Our Personality Has Two Main Components

Years ago, as I delved deeply into who I was and what I liked, I encountered elements of my personality not to my liking. Those elements of my shadow tested my compassion and my self-love. They also provided me with an opportunity to let my pride and ego know who the boss is. (FYI, that would be me.)

In the process of finding my way to self-acceptance, I was able to not only shed light on what I liked, but also start weaving the elements of who I am together in a way that matches the type of person I desire to be. During this time, I encountered some challenges and due to my personal spiritual beliefs, I set out to better understand my personality and how it all worked.

When I considered Spirit as loving and that there were elements of my personality, like my stubbornness, that created challenges for me in my life, I couldn't see how we are just stuck with personality traits. Upon consideration and contemplation, I uncovered a deeper understanding of the nature of human personality.

What I discovered is that we have a *fixed* and *chosen* component to our personality. I uncovered this knowledge through personal experience and observation, so like everything else, put what you read to the test and see if you agree with me.

The Fixed Component

Years ago, I started to cultivate my self-love by taking the time to figure out who I am and what I liked. I tried to put those pieces together to not only create a life I dreamed of, but to create a life that allowed me to be a kind person. My desire to be a "good" person ran into roadblocks when I uncovered certain personality traits within me that challenged my ability to be kind.

It seemed to me that I had two opposing forces within me: my self-love and self-acceptance, and my desire to be kind. For how could I live the life I wanted and still honor my stubbornness?

This confusion led to insight when I considered the situation from the perspective of what I know about Spirit and the human experience. I discovered, after deep consideration and personal testing, that we have certain personality traits that are a part of us because they come from our soul contract.

These traits, both positive and negative, are ones we have chosen in order to facilitate our desires. By having certain personality

CHAPTER 10: MANIFESTATION – HOW IT ALL LOOKS

traits, we create for ourselves scenarios that will provide us the lessons and experiences that we chose to have.

Since we have these fixed personality traits, we can utilize tools like astrology, numerology, and personality tests to uncover elements of who we are and how we operate.

I then further developed my understanding of the fixed component of our personality when I received a past life reading (Conclusion #10- Reincarnation). Following this astounding reading, I decided to make a record of all the past lives I had uncovered, through my own memories and what other psychics had revealed to me over the years.

As I compiled all my known lifetimes, a pattern began to emerge. As soon as my eyes caught sight of it, I took the time to compare the various elements within these past lives and discovered that part of our fixed personality is not the result of necessary traits to fulfill our soul contract, but rather the core of our soul.

I discovered that who you are on a soul level comes to the surface in any lifetime no matter where you are, your gender, or the current focus of your life. Your soul, your higher self, has certain key personality traits that can't be covered by loss of memory or your soul contract.

From these personal moments of contemplation, and by putting my theory to the test, I discovered that parts of our selves are here to stay.

The Chosen Component

But once I uncovered these fixed elements to a person's personality, I was again challenged with how to display self-love and be a kind person. It was upon some further contemplation that I uncovered the second main component to our personality—the chosen element.

What I discovered is that we still get to choose who we are. It's as if the influence of destiny and free will continues to come into play. Our fixed component is linked with our destiny, pieces of ourselves pre-determined before we incarnate into this lifetime.

Our free will, who we choose to be today, is the big picture of who we are. By adding different personality traits as well as learning skills and tools, we can support the wonderful traits within us while managing the more trickster personality traits. In this way, we may honor all of who we are while still deciding how we weave within the world, achieving that desire to be a kind person.

While our fixed personality traits will provide us with the skills or challenges we need to facilitate the lessons and experiences we've chosen for our life, who we are is still our choice. Anyone can be a kind and loving person.

That's key number one: to know who you are, and to choose to continue the journey of self-discovery so that you can identify what will bring happiness into your life for all your days to come.

Love Yourself

The second key is self-love, and this is so, so important. In loving ourselves, we determine the quality of our lives in so many ways. With self-love comes self-worth which will influence our decisions so that they help and support us in building an internal and external world that is healthy and filled with happiness.

Essentially, self-love is going to be that driving force that will get us to pick up our basket, chuck out all our apples, and inspect them one-by-one. It will be the moment-to-moment deciding factor in whether or not we make the choice that is healthiest and best for us, or the one that is easiest.

Self-love supports us as we choose to go against social norms, end dysfunctional relationships, and set out on a different path in life. As we continue on in life and in our healing journey, self-love will steer us away from shame, guilt, and self-judgment and towards compassion, forgiveness, courage, and our dreams.

While self-knowledge will let you know who you are and what you like, self-love will provide you with the push and courage necessary to actually pick and stick with the path that creates a Heart-Centered Life.

Connection to Spirit

Our third key is spiritual connection. As we've discussed, for me, that's Spirit. In understanding Spirit, we come to understand the world and the basics of our human experience. This understanding then becomes our foundation for a personal philosophy.

But a connection with Spirit isn't just to achieve a better understanding; it also determines the quality and condition of your human experience. What I mean by this is that we as human beings don't know everything. We've talked about what our brain is capable of understanding, and how philosophy relies on our ability to understand the world within us and around us.

But I propose that life is capable of such greatness, that it exceeds what our brains are currently capable of comprehending. Because of that, we can be left with so many questions and unknowns that they can become worries, fears, and doubts. At least that's my experience. But does it have to be so?

> **An Apple to Analyze**
> Can you live through a moment where you don't know the answer (unknown) free of panic, worry, or fear? Does fear "have to be" a part of moments where we lack knowledge?

One of the ways we can increase the happiness in our lives is by creating a spiritual connection. Not just by acknowledging Spirit, that sentient being who has created Earth, our soul, and all of existence, but by choosing to build a relationship with that sentient being, Spirit.

By developing a relationship with Spirit, we are then able to say to Spirit, "Hey, I have this question that I don't have the answer to, and rather than spending the next five minutes in a state of panic, I would like to pass this burden onto you. And I'm going to spend the next five minutes enjoying this sunset I am watching."

Here we can see that we are not condemned to live each moment when we lack knowledge in a state of panic or fear. Fear and its seed would like us to, but we don't "have to."

Our relationship with Spirit builds from this understanding: that we are able to and even meant to reach out, so that we can create a life where we don't *have to* just accept panic and pain. We can question it, and in most cases transform the moment into one of happiness by trusting in divine timing, our spirit guides, and Spirit, who know more than we do.

An Apple To Test About Spirit

Conclusion

We can call on Spirit at any time, be it to just talk, to ask for aid, or to release the load we carry so we can spend a moment of our life in happiness.

My Argument

We are talking about Spirit. We are dealing with a sentient being that can transmute energy into a Solar System and has the mental capacity for physics, mathematics, biology, and understands the interwoven nature of souls, planet, and Solar System.

When we consider just who Spirit is and what Spirit has done, we learn that Spirit is capable of being there, guiding and supporting us when we each call out and pray. When you can create a galaxy, being able to connect with each of us on an individual level is not too difficult nor beyond Spirit's capacity.

So, when we call out to Spirit or ask for guidance and support, we are not taking Spirit from someone else. We are utilizing a relationship, an opportunity, and connection to better our lives.

Lastly, if we consider Spirit as loving, then we learn that Spirit would love to hear from us, to know how we're doing, what we love about Earth, and what we find challenging. Spirit loves to hear from loved ones.

What do you think about my argument? Is this an apple you will add to your basket?

With these Three Keys, we possess the structure to cultivate a Path of Happiness. This lifestyle will lead us into a new world of love, where we weave a wonderful life today and help to perpetuate and maintain self-love and this lifestyle into the future.

Breaking Down the Present Moment: Small Picture

While our personalized Path of Happiness creates the overall structure for a Heart-Centered Lifestyle, life is happening in this very moment. As a direct result, our true power in life is tied to the present moment.

As we've seen, if we invest our energy on the past, all we get is an unchanged history. We become really tired, frustrated, and even defeated. If we desire change and healing, we must accomplish this transformation through the decisions we make today.

By choosing to approach the present moment in a healthy manner, we are able to…

- See things as they are, avoiding that assumption trap.
- Love in an authentic and healthy manner because we see things as they are.
- Become aware, so we can do as Teacher #2 did and make decisions in a loving way, creating those teachable moments.
- Make choices through our actions and words that will not only create a happy today but help perpetuate this Path of Happiness moving forward. The big picture (your life; the Path of Happiness) is created by the smaller pictures (present moment choices).

To become a being of love, we first must draw ourselves back into the present. Once we accomplish this, we not only encounter the emotions that we are experiencing, but we bring our minds to the truth of what it is to actively and informatively navigate our lives. We also embrace the journey we are on and our current place in this current cycle.

When you accept the truth of where you are on your journey, you'll no longer see life as a battle or a fight against reality. When we stop fighting, we open up ourselves to experience a Heart-Centered Lifestyle.

What It Looks Like: The Steps

When we encounter a new moment, there are a series of steps that we take to not only live in the moment but to honor the knowledge we have covered in this book. You will first start this process within your consciousness. As you practice and gain skill, you will reach a place where you can address these steps quickly and naturally. They will then become a natural part of your daily life.

Scenario

You have been invited to dinner at a friend's house. You're met at the door and invited in. As your host leads you to the living room you are transitioning into a new moment. As you walk past the threshold and into the living room, these are the steps you will take.

Be in the Present Moment

Rather than allowing your thoughts to wander, become aware of the décor, what people are saying, and how you are feeling. If your thoughts had been occupied as you waited at the front door, make the conscious choice to realign with the present moment.

Avoid Assumptions

As you walk past that threshold and into a new moment, choose to be open. Rather than constructing a story in your mind of what the evening will be like or what people will say and do, choose to avoid the assumptions.

Not only do you save yourself from potential disappointment, confusion, or miscommunication, but you also honor the community that we share. By choosing to remain open you are not handing others a mask (a story of who they are), you are instead letting them show you who they are. This achieves authentic connection and thus an authentic and healthy love.

In addition, by being open, you provide a wounded human being the opportunity to change. Rather than going in thinking and treating someone as that bum, bully, or aggressive person, you are providing them the chance to show you who they are today. Maybe that person is different than who they were before; maybe they have healed and are now a supportive member of our community.

An Apple to Test

Since Volume One, we've been putting apples to the test. These pieces of wisdom have, at times, improved the quality of our lives and, at other times, required us to give up what we thought we knew for something healthier. In this case, we have personally seen the importance of wisdom and the major role it plays in our lives.

Due to the importance that apples (conclusions) play in our lives, I have a new conclusion for you to put to the test.

Conclusion:

Approaching each moment free of assumptions is important.

Argument

As you live your life, your experiences are colored by a conclusion and how you perceive the world changes to reflect this conclusion. Your mind then understands life based on this conclusion and thus supports it.

For example, when we live our lives with an apple of optimism or pessimism, our mind will align itself with this understanding. When we view a situation, the positive or negative attributes will be filtered by our mind, displaying what we're looking for and providing proof that life is grand or horrible.

The danger then lies when we have a conclusion that is wrong (rotten apple). You can end up bringing pain into your life. When we fail to see the full truth of things we can make erroneous choices, feel inaccurate feelings, and compromise our experience of life.

To avoid limiting the possibilities from life, you need to approach each new moment with a clean slate. Life will then either support or contradict your understanding.

Thus, you refine your personal philosophy of life through time and re-write the rules in the moment rather than dragging rotten apples around with you. Choose to test the apples in the moment and move forward wiser and healthier without creating a situation requiring a deep healing journey.

Analyze

Before you even walk past the threshold, you are present and open to what this new moment might be. Once you walk past the threshold and great your friends, you take a moment to get your bearings. Who says what? What does your friend do? Who's in a good mood? Who's changed?

Decide

Now that you have a sense of this new moment, it is time to decide how to act and what to say. For example:
- If your friend's having a bad day, choosing to avoid difficult topics will help facilitate a wonderful evening.
- If your friend acts unchanged, you can choose to remain guarded against a wounded person.
- If your friend has changed, you can choose to talk to them and see who they are now.

Through the knowledge you have gained by saying hello and observing them, you are now in a place to make an informed decision about your choices. These choices will help keep you safe, help you display the characteristics of a kind person (unconditional love plus xenia), help you be there for your friends (philia), and also help you continue to manifest a happy, Heart-Centered Life.

Practice and Learning

Here's the thing about being in the present moment when living a Heart-Centered Lifestyle on a Path of Happiness: it takes practice and learning. Please do not hold yourself to the standard and goal that you will be able to enact these steps right away and all the time. Choose self-love when you approach this skill.

CHAPTER 10: MANIFESTATION – HOW IT ALL LOOKS

I did not start out approaching my day from an ever-present mindfulness, and truthfully, there are still moments in my life where my own emotions and thoughts distract me from following these steps. Yet each time I come back to this approach, I am little bit stronger and more consistent with being present and free of assumptions. As a result, I am able to facilitate an authentic life and make decisions influenced not by habit or my subconscious, but my healthy apples and self-love.

As you begin to learn these steps, you might not be able to enact them at every moment, especially when you've had a long day and are tired. In the moments where your emotions are running high or your entire focus is needed elsewhere, it might not be feasible to slow down and consider the present free of assumptions. Take time and have compassion with yourself. Trust the process.

These steps are wonderful when looking back on past moments in your life. As you study who you were, ask yourself, what apples were guiding your life? What did you not notice about others? These steps can shed light, uncover patterns, and teach you more about yourself so that you can gain greater clarity, forgive, practice self-love, heal, and move on.

Whether it's in the moment or afterwards, please practice self-care and do not demand perfection from yourself. These steps are meant to provide guidance as you move forward in your life, not cause harm.

Learning More

Who I am today started not with wisdom but with ignorance, because before we can know things, we start by not knowing. When we acknowledge our own ignorance, we create a space inside of ourselves to hold the wisdom we have yet to discover.

Within this volume I have attempted to show you the world I live in through my eyes and heart. To teach you the various elements that make up a Heart-Centered Life as a being of love.

While you now possess the skills to create and maintain your Path of Happiness, we don't ever stop learning. Whether it's more about vulnerability from Brené Brown or how to delve into your shadow with shadow work, keep seeking out wisdom.

The assumption fallacy teaches us that we cannot know something until we have been exposed to it. So, what is it that you want to know? What do you need to learn to manifest and create your dream life?

More Resources

If you're interested in learning more, check out these people and works which have guided and inspired me in my life.

- Dr. Brené Brown- on vulnerability, shame, and trust (https://brenebrown.com/)
- Doctors John and Julie Gottman- on relationships (https://www.gottman.com/)
- Dr. Heidi Green- with her book on self-love (https://www.drheidigreen.com/)
- Dr. Dan Siegel – on being in the present moment (awareness) and the human mind (https://drdansiegel.com/)

For even more resources, check out the tools page on my website, where I list in alphabetical order the various resources I have utilized in my life. (https://raemedicinewoman.com/tools/)

Chapter Ten Takeaways: Manifestation– How it All Looks

- We each have a story about who we are.
- How we tell this story influences the quality of our lives as well as the quality of our love.
- Big Picture: We choose to walk a Path of Happiness.
- Small Picture: We live in the present moment, pulling in what we know free of assumptions, to not only create a happy today but to help maintain this lifestyle in the future.
- We never stop learning, so as you live your life and navigate all that you encounter, keep yourself open to new wisdom and tools. When you don't know, avoid the assumption fallacy and instead seek out the knowledge you need and desire.

EPILOGUE

Stepping Into a New World

We live in two realities that not only provide us space to be our complex and individual selves, but also provide us space to share, to acknowledge, utilize, and honor the community we have. When we can take this knowledge of our community and bring it to a conscious level, our egos lose power and stops fighting the natural unity we share here on Earth. As a result, the world we step into is not only loving but supportive.

Much of our thriving human experience comes from our internal world. Our personal philosophy, body, mind, heart, and soul shape not only how we perceive life but also the choices we make, which in turn impact the quality of our lives.

It is then, through this community that we share, that we can support and elevate not just the human experience but life itself, embodying the potential and beauty that Spirit wove into creation.

I sat at my kitchen table to complete this book and as I sat here, I was reminded of the voice I have, and with you reading these words, I am heard. This is a very powerful thing.

During the course of this book I have set out to remove the veil that has obscured my world and invite you into it. To not only show you and teach you the elements of this world but impart the feeling of it as well.

EPILOGUE

Now here we are at the end and I want my voice to speak one last powerful truth. So here it is.

You matter.

If you take nothing else from this book, take this truth with you: that you are special and loved no matter what you see when you look in the mirror or who you love in life.

To live a Heart-Centered Life merely means to choose love with each path you take. That when you encounter people or need to make a decision about life, you choose a path of love. Put this idea and emotion into action, love yourself, love your family, love those lost and in pain, and love life. For we all matter.

BIBLIOGRAPHY

Aronson, Polina. *Which Romantic Regime Do You Follow?*. http://aeon.co/magazine/psychology/which-romantic-regime-do-you-follow/. 30 October 2015. pg. 2

Brown, Brené. *The Anatomy of Trust*. SuperSoul Sessions. https://brenebrown.com/videos/anatomy-trust-video/. Oprah Winfrey Network. 2015. UCLA's Royce Hall. 19:11 – 19:20

Brown, Brené. *The Power of Vulnerability*. www.ted.com. TED Talks. 3 January 2011. 3:22 – 3:30, 8:55 – 9:06

Brown, Brené. *Listening to Shame*. www.ted.com. TED Talks. 16 March 2012. 4:00 – 5:07, 6:00 – 6:05

Cannon, Walter. *Bodily Changes in Pain, Hunger, Fear, and Rage*. 1st edition. New York and London, D. Appleton and Co., 1915

Carl Jung. https://en.wikipedia.org/wiki/Carl_Jung. Wikipedia. 24 August 2021

Conservation of Mass. https://en.wikipedia.org/wiki/Conservation_of_mass. Wikipedia. 1 August 2021

Declaration of Independence: A Transcription. National Archives, U.S. National Archives and Records Administration, 15 September 2021, https://www.archives.gov/founding-docs/declaration-transcript.

Descartes, René. *The Method, Meditations on First Philosophy*. Translated by Veitch, John. 1901

Greek Words For Love. https://en.wikipedia.org/wiki/Greek_words_for_love. Wikipedia. 30 July 2021.

J.M.K.C. Donev et al. (2020). *Energy Education - Law of conservation of energy* [Online]. Available: **https://energyeducation.ca/encyclopedia/Law_of_ conservation_of_energy**. [Accessed: August 29, 2021].

"Meraki." *The Meaning of Meraki.*
https://themeaningofmerakicom.wordpress.com/.

Miracle on 34th Street. Directed by George Seaton. 20th Century Fox. 1947.

Rojviroj, Wanee. Punyahotra, Vichit. Sittiprapaporn, Wichian. Sarikaphuti, Ariya. *Study of Brain Activity Analysis of Deep Breathing.* Mae Fa Luang University. pg. 6

Tseng, J., Poppenk, J. Brain meta-state transitions demarcate thoughts across task contexts exposing the mental noise of trait neuroticism. *Nat Commun* 11, 3480 (2020). https://doi.org/10.1038/s41467-020-17255-9

"vulnerability." *Merriam-Webster.com.* Merriam-Webster, 2021. Web. 26 August 2021.

ACKNOWLEDGEMENTS

Having undergone the publishing process twice I cannot express enough how writing is a collaborative work. While the initial process starts with an idea and long hours sitting lost in thought, as your hands type away, what follows is nothing less than a connection between people.

For as you write, you find friends and family who will sit and listen to you as you hash out the order of information, the content, and the manner in which you will share your wisdom. For this step I have my mother most of all to thank. Whether it was a listening ear or taking the time to read my work, she put in long hours as well to help bring this work to the finish line.

Following this process of writing and re-writing, it's time for an editor to step in, not only with knowledge pertaining to grammar and phrasing, but an unobscured eye to point out the redundancies and indecipherable sections. For this step I must thank Lia, who also worked with me on Volume One. Her insight and compassion create a special blend of editorial correction and protection for this author's exposed heart.

Once the manuscript has been edited, revised, and reviewed the work is finished and it's time to put it into book format. For this step I have Geoff to thank who not only created the cover art, the necessary diagrams, but also formatted the interior of the book and prepared it for publication. Like Lia, Geoff has been with me since the beginning, and brings artistic insight, heart, and a beautiful blend of his ideas and my own. Which creates the finished product that you now see.

Any book worth its salt is a representation of a number of people. What you see before you could not be without the aid of my wonderful team. While the process starts within my mind and takes me hours to put down in a somewhat coherent manner, this process is not a journey one takes alone. But rather is imbued with the energies and thoughts of a community. For them I send my thanks and appreciation for their aid and support.

ABOUT THE AUTHOR

Rae Beecher is a medicine woman, and through her writing, energy healing, and tarot reading shares wisdom and healing with the world. With her debut book in *The Human Experience Series, Volume I: What is the Human Experience?* she began a healing journey to cultivate a healthy personal philosophy. In her sequel she continues on this healing journey designed to help educate and lead the reader to a personalized thriving human experience.

Rae Beecher lives in Washington State and enjoys spending time with friends and family and pursuing her different hobbies, including music, photography, cooking, and baking. She especially loves traveling around her home in search of Mother Earth's many beauties.

www.ingramcontent.com/pod-product-compliance
Lightning Source LLC
Chambersburg PA
CBHW030903080526
44589CB00010B/127